ALSO BY AMANDA RETTKE

Surprise-Inside Cakes

HOMESTEAD

Recipes

MIDWESTERN INSPIRATIONS, FAMILY FAVORITES, AND PEARLS OF WISDOM FROM A SASSY HOME COOK

AMANDA RETTKE

wm

WILLIAM MORROW

An Imprint of HarperCollinsPublishers

TO CHAD—LIFE IS BETTER WITH YOU

CONTENTS

INTRODUCTION

INTRODUCTION

I AM
homesteader

I **HAVE BEEN FOOD BLOGGING FOR OVER A DECADE.** My first ever blog was named *i am mommy* and it was about, you guessed it, being a mom. I knew nothing about baking or cooking (or momming, for that matter) and was forced into the task by having to feed a hardworking husband and kids. As I started to share my baked goods online, I decided that I didn't want recipes clogging up my precious mommy blog, so I started *i am baker*. That hasty decision ended up changing my life by introducing me to a world of dessert and amazing new friends, and it gave me an opportunity to tap into a skill set I never knew I possessed: baking stuff and making people laugh.

Speaking of humor, mine is self-deprecating and observational. As a Midwesterner, born and raised, behaviors from around the country never cease to baffle and delight me. I thought *Valley Girl* was just a movie, not a way of talking that actually existed in the world. The first live video I ever did on Facebook was inundated with comments like "I love your accent!" and "You remind me of that movie *Fargo*!" An accent? Well, apparently I talked funny, at least according to the rest of the country. And acted funny and ate weird things like hot dish and lefse. As a small-town girl trying to make an impact on the World Wide Web, it occurred to me that if I was going to make any impact at all, it would have to be at my own expense, which just so happened to fit right into my already self-deprecating personality.

The first "character" I ever posted was in 2011. She was named Aunt Inga. She had a hubby named Sven and said things like "you betcha" and "dontcha know." She was based on the family I loved and language I was familiar with. She paved the way for Shirley (more on that in a bit).

About eight years ago, well into my food-blogging career, my husband and I bought a fifteen-acre property in rural Minnesota. He grew up farming and knew how to garden, can, and build things. I decided I wanted to dive headfirst into homesteading and raise chickens, ducks, guinea fowl—and maybe goats and pigs someday. With zero experience or knowledge under my belt, I wanted to figure out how to have a garden big enough to sustain the family even throughout a long, cold Minnesota winter. We have achieved those goals thus far—and that love of homesteading led to my starting a new website called i am homesteader. Lots of savory slow-cooking recipes—hot dish, meat and potatoes, and all the things we actually eat as a family of seven. I love my blogs and website and what they represent and am thankful for the impact they have made on our lives.

SHIRLEY

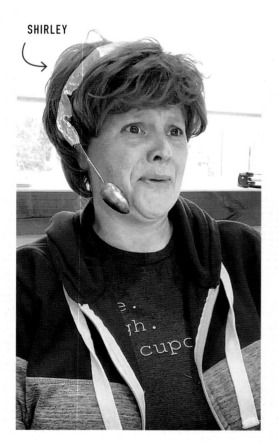

But I'm going to tell you something that I probably shouldn't tell you: I didn't write this book for the reasons you might think, and I am not your average homesteader.

Up until 2020, I had desperately wanted to share a cookbook that *everyone* would love, that would have recipes that *everyone* would enjoy, that would be overwhelming in a fantastic culinary kind of way. I wanted to win awards and be recognized and have people sending me letters ten years from now telling me that it is still one of their favorite books. Big, bold, ambitious dreams.

But everything changed—in pretty dramatic ways—during the pandemic.

I stayed at home for fourteen months (literally) and ended up going a little stir-crazy. I created a character called Shirley on my Instagram page. She works for the Your Content Is Terrible Hotline, answering calls about terrible content on the internet. This was inspired by feedback I had gotten about my own website. It was me venting in a very passive-aggressive way—but people seemed to think it was funny!

All of a sudden I had more attention than I could have ever dreamed of. Famous people were following me, reporters were calling me, and production companies were asking if I wanted to do my own TV show on the best networks.

Um—*Yes! Dream come true!*

After months of negotiations with my dream producers and network, I did the unthinkable: I walked away from that opportunity.

Something important had occurred to me through that process of negotiating my worth (man, was that a humbling experience): Fame and notoriety were not as important to me as I had thought. In fact, they were the *opposite* of what I saw in my future. I didn't tell many people, because I thought the world would see my decision as foolish. And I honestly understand why people would think that. The truth was, it wasn't my dream.

It occurred to me in a loud, crazy, no-doubt-about-it kind of way that I *had* everything I wanted right now. I didn't need to reinvent the wheel and hope that folks would see my value as a food blogger and content creator. And I realized that the recipes I wanted to share in this book didn't have to be 100 percent innovative. But they did have to mean something, even if only to me.

So this book, the one you are holding in your hands, is the furthest thing from an attempt to make it for *everyone*. It simply contains the recipes that my family makes and loves. These recipes are comfort food. They are heavily influenced by my midwestern roots, with a mix of baking creativity. Lots of folks don't have any idea how fantastic and crazy the food is here in the Midwest—salads made of dessert. Hot dish for any time of the day and every occasion. Bar recipes that get passed around to every lady at the church for generations. There's nothing fancy about it. And we don't eat "from the land" for every meal. I am the first to admit that while I am obsessed with my cream cheese coffee cake, my kids often start the day with cereal because I couldn't get my act together in time to make them breakfast. For five days in a row. Every week.

I sincerely hope that you do love these recipes and that there is something in this book you can enjoy with your family. I hope it will encourage big family meals where stories are shared and memories are made. And that after making something from this book, you'll carry with you the memories of the best snickerdoodle cookie you ever had and, most important, the people you shared it with.

MEET THE *family*

ALL MY KIDS MAKE ME LAUGH, but Olivia makes me belly-laugh. The way she can drop a one-liner with innocence in her eyes—except for that little sparkle of devious delight—makes her my favorite. The way she sees the world and how she interprets things never fail to bring me joy! Like when she asks me, "Do I really have to wear sleeves on my legs, Mom?" Yes, sweet child, pants are necessary in February in Minnesota.

Olivia is passionate about food. All food. She will try anything and she will enjoy it, even if she doesn't. Every meal ends with "That was the best meal I've ever had in my entire life, Mom"—and I think she means it.

I can't include her opinion when testing recipes because she would rather stub her toe than ever tell me she didn't like something. One time I made an incredibly ugly cake. It was a complete decorating fail. She ran up to me and said, "Huggy!" (because she needs a minimum of 397 hugs a day), then, "It's okay, Mom. It's pretty in my mind." She sure is great to have around when my confidence needs a boost!

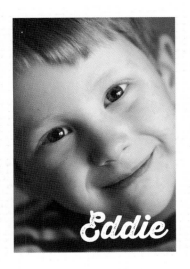

EDDIE—MY DEAR, SWEET EDDIE. Probably my pickiest eater, but that is of my own creation. From the moment he was born, he had this gorgeous red hair and bright blue eyes. I tell him I love his hair every time he is in my presence. That is not an exaggeration. Out of five kids, he is the only redhead!

He is set up on a pedestal and I am constantly telling him how special he is, how only 1 to 2 percent of the population has red hair and only .17 percent of the population has red hair *and* blue eyes. He is my favorite child. He's *smart as heck*. Remembers everything he's ever heard, can recite Bible verses better than I, and could probably skip ahead three grades if he didn't love his friends in his class so much. But he doesn't like tomatoes. Early on, I told him that was okay, he didn't have to like all foods, just try them at least once. *Although* maybe I didn't make him try them . . . he is my favorite after all.

AUDREY HAS BEEN HELPING ME with my food blogs and is turning out to be quite the baker. She makes cookies and cakes and has such amazing ideas for new cookie creations. Sometimes I look at Audrey and wonder how I got so lucky as a mom. She is so beautiful, inside and out. But the inside part is what constantly amazes me.

I love heart-to-hearts with Audrey. She has an ability to be raw and vulnerable, and that is something I have never, ever possessed. She's twelve going on thirty and yet sees the world through an innocent and hopeful lens. I hope that she keeps those attributes forever, as they are such a beautiful expression of her faith and her capacity to love. Audrey is my favorite, my hope for the future, and will probably contribute to my going completely gray. For now, for six more precious years, I am going to hold on tight to her because being around Audrey makes me a better person. I can't wait to someday call my daughter my friend.

DID YOU EVER HAVE A CHILD who is a born leader? That's my Colton. He is a firstborn, so that explains a lot, but he also has this natural self-confidence, which inspires me like crazy. He is sixteen, handsome, six feet tall, has no desire to get his driver's license, wears Stormy Kromer hats, and wants to be a poultryman someday. Colton marches to the beat of his own drum. I have no idea where he gets this innate confidence and complete lack of concern for what others think about him.

He has been a huge help for my business, working after school and all throughout the summer. He is an official taste tester for my food blogs because I know he will tell me the truth *and* offer up advice on how to make it better. He's clearly my favorite child. The quintessential firstborn, the trusty, dependable one. He still gives me a hug every single day and is the first to look at me randomly and say, "Need a hug, Mom? It looks like you need a hug." And I always do.

WHEN PARKER WAS A BABY, strangers would stop me in stores and say that he was the most beautiful baby they'd ever seen. As his mom, I already knew that, *of course*, but it sure is nice to hear.

Parker is the opposite of me . . . quiet, thoughtful, and so careful with his words. When he talks, we all stop to listen intently, because we know it will be impactful. His unique sensitive demeanor makes him my favorite child. And I know that when I let him start dating at twenty-five, he will be a ladies' man—all the girls will be drawn to his amazing listening skills and charming smile. Oh my word, I just gave myself a heart attack. Dating is officially out of the question until I am dead.

I LUCKED OUT IN THE HUSBAND DEPARTMENT. Chad is handsome, kind, a great friend to all, and a devoted son, brother, father, and husband. Hugely successful with his chosen career and as calm and matter of fact as they come. When folks say "opposites attract," they aren't kidding. We are nothing alike. Chad gets along with everyone. I pick fights with imaginary people and scream at anyone who has ever been lucky enough to be driving on the road at the same time I am.

We were fortunate enough to be able to retire him a few years ago, and the kids have absolutely thrived with him being home. Get this—he does homework with the kids and doesn't even yell. Like, he's *patient*. What's that all about? He is the reason I don't go off on the world every five seconds—I tell him my woes and he listens, then calmly says, "It is what it is." Then I mimic "It is what it is" in a sarcastic, whiny voice and sulk until it sinks in that he's right and I can't change anything about anyone else.

You know what else Chad is amazing at? Guessing things. I will come in after a twelve-hour day and say, "Guess what?," and he'll guess it. *Who does that?* If I'd been about to say, "Alligators have seven legs now," he would have already guessed. Sigh. I love that man. But he probably already guessed that.

UFFDA

Having grown up with this word, I really didn't know it wasn't widely used until the internet made fun of me. And once that happened, I made it my mission to say it as often as possible. I'm stubborn like that.

You may be wondering, what does *uffda* even mean? It's *so simple*. We Minnesotans use that word when we are surprised, upset, or tired; when it is too cold or too hot outside, when something bad happens; when we want to let Southerners know just how northern we are; when someone guesses a bad letter on *Wheel of Fortune*; and most important, when there is an emotional response required in hard conversations. If a Minnesotan responds with an *uffda*, they probably care very deeply about you and your situation, and that is their way of expressing it. That or they just got bit by a mosquito.

HOMESTEADING

If you look up the definition of *homesteading*, you'll probably realize we don't quite fit it. We aren't self-sufficient. I love having a grocery store ten minutes away and definitely love Amazon delivering anything I may need right to my doorstep, even if it often takes two to seven days to get here. I also really, really love electricity. Summers in Minnesota are often very hot, and I would be a mess without air-conditioning. I consider myself "naturally insulated," dontcha know. I also love my stand mixer and oven and don't want to resort to exclusively campfire cooking *just yet*.

We do, however, garden and preserve food, raise fowl, keep bees, and own a tractor that we use all year long. I make a mean salve from the acres of dandelions, and we feed the birds with our giant sunflowers.

The kids have a firm grasp of the circle of life and have helped build a chicken coop and an outhouse; they've stacked wood for days and know the proper protocol should they see a bear. (Yes, we have seen them around—even on our deck!) When it comes to recipes from the homestead, many utilize the bounty of the garden as well as the animals we raise. We collect eggs daily from our free-range chickens and raise meat hens for butchering, which we also do ourselves right here on the property.

We are always looking for opportunities to be more self-sufficient and to teach our kids survival tools should they suddenly find themselves alone in the middle of a forest and in need of food and shelter. It could totally happen.

BREAKFAST

TRUTH BE TOLD, my husband is the official breakfast maker in the family. He contributed a few amazing recipes to the book and I am so thankful. Baked goods are my specialty—you won't find a better banana muffin anywhere—but savory is his. Pulled Pork Hash, Homemade Sausage Patties with Jalapeño and Cheddar, and Ham and Cheese Egg Bake are from his brain and upbringing.

Breakfast is the only meal of the day that I can indulge in and not feel guilty after. You have the whole day ahead of you to take the stairs instead of the elevator, park far away from the grocery store to get a few steps in, or take a run later to burn off those extra glorious calories. Of course I don't do any of those things, but I *could*.

BUTTERMILK PANCAKES WITH BLUEBERRY SYRUP

I had to resist the urge to put my *real* recipe in this book. The only difference is quantity, but it's a big difference for us. We quadruple this recipe. My family of seven devour as many as they can, but there are always a few left over. Those are designated for day snacking and the chickens. Our chickens love pancakes and will jump for joy, quite literally, when they see us walking to the coop with a stack. So while, yes, these pancakes are amazing for humans and you will love them, and they are worth trying next time you decide to treat the family to a hot breakfast, they are also fantastic for any feathery friends you might also consider family.

PREP TIME: 20 minutes • **COOK TIME:** 10 minutes • **MAKES 8 PANCAKES**

1. In a large bowl, stir together the flour, baking powder, salt, and sugar.

2. In a medium bowl, whisk the buttermilk, egg, and melted butter. Pour the buttermilk mixture into the flour mixture and stir until just combined, taking care not to overmix.

3. Melt about a tablespoon of butter in an electric griddle over medium heat. Drop about ¼ cup of batter into the skillet and let the batter expand. When bubbles form on the edges (about 2 minutes), flip the pancake and continue cooking until golden brown. Repeat with the remaining batter, greasing the griddle with more butter as necessary.

4. Serve warm with blueberry syrup.

1½ cups (188 g) all-purpose flour

3½ teaspoons baking powder

½ teaspoon kosher salt

¼ cup (50 g) granulated sugar

1¼ cups (300 ml) buttermilk

1 large egg

3 tablespoons unsalted butter, melted and cooled, plus more for the griddle

Blueberry Syrup (recipe follows), for serving

Blueberry Syrup

PREP TIME: 5 minutes • **COOK TIME:** 20 minutes

3 cups (570 g) fresh or frozen blueberries

3 tablespoons freshly squeezed lemon juice

⅓ cup (67 g) granulated sugar

1 tablespoon cornstarch

1. Place a medium saucepan over medium-low heat. Add the blueberries, lemon juice, sugar, and ⅓ cup (80 ml) water to the saucepan. Bring to a gentle boil, stirring occasionally, until the sugar has completely dissolved and the blueberries have softened.

2. Meanwhile, in a small bowl, whisk the cornstarch with 2 tablespoons water until dissolved. Add the mixture to the blueberries and stir. Gently boil until thickened, 5 to 10 minutes. Remove from the heat (the sauce will thicken further as it cools).

3. Store the syrup in an airtight container in the refrigerator for up to 2 weeks.

HAM AND CHEESE EGG BAKE

I was first introduced to egg bakes by my mother-in-law, Patty. On a beautiful Saturday morning more than twenty years ago, she served one to my husband and me for breakfast. I didn't want to reveal my ignorance, so I didn't say anything, but I sure did show them I was a "healthy" eater. From that moment on we have incorporated egg bakes into our breakfast routine.

The beauty of this recipe? You can make it ahead of time, and you can easily modify it with whatever ingredients you have on hand. Sausage and Gruyère? Go for it. Salmon and dill? Um, yes, please.

PREP TIME: 20 minutes • **CHILL TIME:** 8 hours • **COOK TIME:** 1 hour • **MAKES 12 SERVINGS**

1. Grease a 9 × 13-inch baking dish with nonstick spray.

2. Arrange half the bread in the prepared baking dish. Top the bread with half of the diced ham and half the cheese. Add the remaining cubed bread, then ham, and finally cheese.

3. In a large bowl, whisk the eggs. Add the milk, ground mustard, salt, and pepper and stir to combine. Pour the egg mixture evenly over the layers of bread, ham, and cheese.

4. Cover the baking dish with foil and refrigerate for 8 to 12 hours to let the egg mixture absorb into the bread.

5. When ready to bake, preheat the oven to 350°F.

6. Bake, covered in the foil, for 45 minutes. Remove the foil and bake for 15 minutes more, or until the center no longer jiggles.

7. Let the egg bake sit for 5 minutes, then cut into squares and serve.

8. Store leftovers in an airtight container in the refrigerator for 2 or 3 days.

Nonstick spray

12 cups ½-inch French bread cubes

2 cups (270 g) finely diced ham

2 cups (226 g) shredded cheddar cheese

12 large eggs

2 cups (480 ml) whole milk

2 teaspoons ground mustard

1 teaspoon kosher salt

½ teaspoon freshly ground black pepper

BUTTERMILK BISCUITS

Growing up in the northern Midwest means that, culinarily speaking, I'm not supposed to be an expert on biscuits. That's a southern specialty. And I can agree to some extent; I didn't grow up at my grandma's side, watching her make biscuits from scratch. But as a food blogger, I've tested more recipes than I can count, and I finally settled on the one recipe that was perfect every time—it bakes up light and fluffy and, most important, is just as good on day two. I often double the recipe on a big sheet pan, as the kids seem insistent on eating food every single day.

The secret to these biscuits is grating the cold butter, then adding more butter right out of the oven. So basically the secret is not a big secret—it's just a lot of butter.

PREP TIME: 10 minutes • **COOK TIME:** 12 to 16 minutes • **MAKES 12 BISCUITS**

1. Preheat the oven to 450°F. Line a sheet pan with parchment paper.

2. Using the fine side of your grater, grate the butter onto a separate piece of parchment paper. Place the paper with the butter in the freezer while you prepare the remaining ingredients.

3. In a large bowl, whisk the flour, sugar, baking soda, and baking powder. Using a fork, incorporate the grated butter into the dry ingredients. Pour in the buttermilk and stir until mostly combined, taking care not to overwork the dough.

4. Place the dough on a work surface and use your hands to push it together, gathering up any dry bits and pressing them into the dough. Add some flour underneath it if the counter is getting sticky. Press the dough into a flat square about 1½ inches thick. Fold over once and press down. Fold over again and press down. Fold over a third time and press the dough to 1½ inches thick.

5. Press a biscuit cutter, round cookie cutter, or tall water glass into the dough and place each biscuit onto the prepared sheet pan.

6. Bake for 12 to 16 minutes, until the tops are golden brown.

7. Remove the biscuits from the oven and brush with melted butter. Serve immediately. (If you're serving later, you can brush with more melted butter right before serving.)

8. Leftovers can be covered and stored at room temperature for 1 or 2 days or in the refrigerator for up to 1 week.

1 cup (2 sticks / 227 g) cold salted butter

4 cups (500 g) all-purpose flour, plus more for the work surface

2 tablespoons granulated sugar

½ teaspoon baking soda

2 tablespoons baking powder

2 cups (480 ml) buttermilk

2 tablespoons melted salted butter, for brushing

SAUSAGE AND GRAVY BISCUITS

If you've made Buttermilk Biscuits (page 9), now it's time to make one heckuva fantastic gravy. I have to echo the sentiment of a long line of home cooks who say, "It's hard to measure the ingredients for gravy; you eyeball it as you go." We most often make sausage gravy in the fall and winter, as it's so hearty and satisfying. And truth be told, I don't always add sage or marjoram, as exhaustion is a common mom trait and I just want to get my sweet family fed. But when I opt to follow the recipe, I'm always delighted by the addition of the extra seasoning. It really does give it something special.

PREP TIME: 15 minutes • **COOK TIME:** 20 minutes • **MAKES 6 SERVINGS**

1. In a large bowl, combine the kosher salt, seasoned salt, black pepper, sage, crushed red pepper flakes, marjoram, and cloves. Add the ground sausage and mix well.

2. In a large skillet over medium-high heat, cook the pork mixture until browned, or until the internal temperature of the pork is 160°F, about 8 minutes. Reduce the heat to medium. Do not drain. Add the flour and stir until the sausage is coated. Pour in the milk, stir, and cook for 10 to 12 minutes, until thickened, stirring often. You may want to add more milk (up to 2 more cups) until the gravy reaches your desired consistency.

3. Serve over the biscuits.

1 teaspoon kosher salt

1 teaspoon Lawry's Seasoned Salt

½ teaspoon freshly ground black pepper

¼ teaspoon ground sage

¼ teaspoon crushed red pepper flakes

Pinch of ground marjoram

Pinch of ground cloves

1 pound (454 g) ground pork sausage

⅓ cup (42 g) all-purpose flour

3 cups (720 ml) whole milk, plus more as needed

½ recipe Buttermilk Biscuits (page 9)

BLUEBERRY COFFEE CAKE

I don't think I'll ever stop being delighted at the idea of cake for breakfast. When I was growing up, my folks would treat us with store-bought coffee cake on the weekends, and it was like Christmas on a Saturday. When I became a food blogger, I started to turn all those wonderful memories into from-scratch versions. This coffee cake can't be considered a healthy breakfast option, but it should be added to the list of family must-makes when it comes to creating fantastic memories and traditions.

PREP TIME: 10 minutes • **COOK TIME:** 55 to 60 minutes • **MAKES 12 SERVINGS**

1. Preheat the oven to 350°F. Grease a 9 × 13-inch baking dish with nonstick spray.

2. **MAKE THE CAKE:** In a large bowl, combine the flour, baking powder, and salt.

3. In the bowl of a stand mixer fitted with the paddle attachment or in a large bowl using a handheld mixer on high speed, cream the butter and granulated sugar until fluffy, 2 to 3 minutes. Add the eggs, milk, oil, and vanilla. Mix on low for about 1 minute. Add the flour mixture to the butter mixture and mix on medium for 30 seconds, or until the ingredients are just incorporated. Remove the bowl from the mixer and fold in the blueberries.

4. Spread the batter in the prepared baking dish.

5. **MAKE THE CRUMBLE:** Using a food processor or in a medium bowl using a fork or your hands, combine the brown sugar, flour, cinnamon, and cold butter chunks, breaking the butter into pieces no larger than a pea. Spread the crumble over the batter.

6. Bake for 55 to 60 minutes. If the top starts to brown, cover the coffee cake with foil. The cake is done when a toothpick inserted into the center comes out with a few crumbs but no wet batter clinging to it. Everyone's oven is different, so make sure the cake is done before removing.

7. **MAKE THE GLAZE:** Place the confectioners' sugar in a medium bowl and whisk in a few drops of milk at a time until it reaches drizzling consistency.

8. Drizzle the glaze over the warm cake and serve.

9. Leftovers can be stored in an airtight container in the refrigerator for up to 1 week.

CAKE

Nonstick spray

4 cups (500 g) all-purpose flour

1 tablespoon baking powder

½ teaspoon kosher salt

1 cup (2 sticks / 227 g) unsalted butter, at room temperature

2 cups (400 g) granulated sugar

4 large eggs, at room temperature

1 cup (240 ml) whole milk

¼ cup (60 ml) vegetable oil

2 teaspoons vanilla extract

2 to 3 cups (570 g) fresh or frozen blueberries

CRUMBLE

⅓ cup (75 g) packed light brown sugar

¼ cup (31 g) all-purpose flour

½ teaspoon ground cinnamon

3 tablespoons cold unsalted butter, cut into chunks

GLAZE

½ cup (63 g) confectioners' sugar

About 2 tablespoons whole milk

CREAM CHEESE COFFEE CAKE

I created this recipe based on a giant muffin that was served at my first waitressing job. It was a family-style restaurant called Randy's located in Fargo, North Dakota. The menu also included lutefisk and lefsa with a free salad bar, but I won't be sharing those recipes. Loaded with cream cheese and with the softest crumb, that muffin was my favorite thing on the earth for at least two years. It melted in the mouth. And rest assured, this coffee cake will too.
See the photo on page 16.

PREP TIME: 15 minutes • **COOK TIME:** 50 to 55 minutes • **MAKES 9 SERVINGS**

CRUMBLE

Nonstick spray (or parchment paper)

½ cup (1 stick / 113 g) cold unsalted butter, cubed

¾ cup (94 g) all-purpose flour

⅓ cup (42 g) confectioners' sugar

CREAM CHEESE FILLING

Two 8-ounce (454 g total) packages cream cheese, at room temperature

1 cup (200 g) granulated sugar

COFFEE CAKE

2 cups (250 g) cake flour

½ teaspoon kosher salt

2 teaspoons baking powder

½ cup (1 stick / 113 g) unsalted butter, at room temperature

¾ cup (150 g) granulated sugar

2 large eggs, at room temperature

2 teaspoons vanilla extract

½ cup (120 ml) whole milk

1. Preheat the oven to 325°F. Grease a 9 × 13-inch baking dish with nonstick spray or line it with parchment paper.

2. **MAKE THE CRUMBLE:** Using a food processor, fork, or your clean hands, combine the butter, flour, and confectioners' sugar in a bowl, breaking up the butter into pieces no larger than the size of a pea. There should not be any loose flour remaining. Refrigerate until ready to use.

3. **MAKE THE CREAM CHEESE FILLING:** In the bowl of a stand mixer fitted with the paddle attachment or in a large bowl using a handheld mixer, combine the cream cheese and granulated sugar on high speed until smooth and creamy, 2 to 4 minutes. Set aside.

4. **MAKE THE COFFEE CAKE:** Into a medium bowl, sift together the flour, salt, and baking powder. Set aside.

5. In the bowl of a stand mixer fitted with the paddle attachment or in a large bowl using a handheld mixer, combine the butter and granulated sugar on medium-high speed until light and fluffy, 2 to 3 minutes. Scrape down the bowl as needed. With the mixer on low, add the eggs, vanilla, and milk. Mix on low until combined, about 30 seconds. Add the dry ingredients and mix on low until just combined, 1 to 2 minutes. Remove the bowl from the mixer and scrape down the sides with a rubber spatula.

6. **ASSEMBLE AND BAKE:** Spread half the coffee cake batter into the prepared pan. Spoon half the cream cheese mixture over the top and spread it out with a spatula, getting it into every corner. It's okay if the cream cheese and batter combine slightly. Top with the remaining batter, then the remaining cream cheese mixture. Evenly sprinkle the crumble over the cream cheese.

7. Bake for 50 to 55 minutes. If the top starts to brown, cover the coffee cake with foil. The cake is done when a toothpick inserted into the center comes out with a few crumbs but no wet batter clinging to it. Everyone's oven is different, so make sure the cake is done before removing. Set the coffee cake aside to cool slightly.

8. **MAKE THE GLAZE:** In a medium bowl, mix together the butter, cream cheese, vanilla, confectioners' sugar, and milk. Add more milk, if necessary, to thin the glaze and reach the desired consistency.

9. Drizzle the glaze over the warm coffee cake and serve.

10. Leftovers can be stored in an airtight container in the refrigerator for 1 or 2 days.

GLAZE

¼ cup (½ stick / 57 g) unsalted butter, at room temperature

2 tablespoons (28 g) cream cheese

½ teaspoon vanilla extract

¾ cup (95 g) confectioners' sugar

¼ cup (60 ml) whole milk, plus more as needed

CREAM CHEESE COFFEE CAKE, PAGE 14

OVERNIGHT CARAMEL ROLLS, PAGE 18

OVERNIGHT CARAMEL ROLLS

I *love* caramel rolls. I do *not* love waking up at the crack of dawn and making them. By the time the rolls are done, I have eaten a bowl of cereal and a banana and had three cups of coffee. Whoops. This is my solution: I make them the day before and then pop them in the fridge. In the morning just turn on the oven (literally—you don't even have to preheat it) and pop them in, and you're minutes away from *giant* caramel roll deliciousness. Oh, did I forget to mention they are *giant*? You don't have to make six—you can make twelve—but let me tell you something. When you plop a giant caramel in front of your sweet family, their eyes will grow, their smiles will appear, and you just might have the best family day ever.
See the photo on page 17.

PREP TIME: 30 minutes • **RESTING TIME:** 90 minutes • **CHILLING TIME:** 1 hour, plus overnight •
COOK TIME: 45 to 50 minutes • **MAKES 6 ROLLS**

DOUGH

2 cups (480 ml) whole milk

½ cup (120 ml) vegetable oil

½ cup (100 g) granulated sugar

2¼ teaspoons (1 packet) active dry yeast

4½ cups (563 g) all-purpose flour, plus more as needed

1½ teaspoons kosher salt

½ teaspoon baking powder

½ teaspoon baking soda

CARAMEL SAUCE

½ cup (1 stick / 114 g) unsalted butter, melted

1 cup (200 g) firmly packed light brown sugar

¼ cup (60 ml) honey

¼ cup (85 g) light corn syrup

1 teaspoon vanilla extract

1 teaspoon kosher salt

1. **MAKE THE DOUGH:** Heat the milk in a medium bowl in the microwave for 2 to 2½ minutes, until the temperature reaches 110°F. Add in the oil and sugar and stir until dissolved.

2. Sprinkle the yeast over the warm milk mixture and let sit for 1 minute.

3. Place 4 cups of the flour in a large bowl. Pour the milk and yeast mixture over the flour and stir until just combined. It should be wet, sticky, and warm. Cover with a kitchen towel and let sit in a warm place for 1 hour.

4. Remove the towel and add the salt, baking powder, baking soda, and the remaining ½ cup flour. Knead on a clean countertop dusted with flour until all the ingredients are incorporated, about 5 minutes. (If you use a large enough bowl, you can knead the ingredients right in the bowl.) If the dough is too sticky, add more flour, a tablespoon at a time.

5. Cover and chill for 1 hour.

6. **MAKE THE CARAMEL SAUCE:** In a medium saucepan over medium heat, melt the butter. Add the brown sugar, honey, corn syrup, vanilla, and salt. Simmer for 8 to 10 minutes, until the sauce has thickened.

7. Pour the caramel sauce into a 9 × 13-inch glass baking dish. Set aside.

8. **ASSEMBLE AND FILL THE ROLLS:** On a large floured surface, roll the dough into a 30 × 10-inch rectangle. Use a clean hand to spread the soft butter over the surface of the dough, making sure to evenly cover all of it, right up to the edges. Sprinkle the dough with the brown sugar and then the cinnamon.

9. Starting on one short side, roll up the dough in a jelly-roll fashion. Cut the roll crosswise into 6 equal slices and set aside. (To get even slices, cut the roll in half at the center, then cut each half into 3 more pieces.) Place the rolls cut side down in the baking dish on top of the caramel sauce.

10. Cover the baking dish with plastic wrap and refrigerate overnight.

11. **THE NEXT DAY:** Set the oven to 350°F, uncover the rolls, and immediately place the baking dish into the oven. (Do not let the oven preheat—the rolls will rise as the oven heats up.) Bake the rolls for 45 to 50 minutes, to an internal temperature of 190°F. Check them after 30 minutes. If the rolls are starting to get too dark, cover them with foil.

12. Invert the rolls onto a large serving platter, caramel side up. Serve warm.

13. Leftovers can be stored in an airtight container in the refrigerator for 1 or 2 days.

DOUGH FILLING

½ cup (1 stick / 114 g) salted butter, very soft

1 cup (200 g) packed light brown sugar

2 tablespoons ground cinnamon

BAKERY-STYLE BLUEBERRY MUFFINS

Blueberries are my favorite fruit. *All-time favorite.* I can eat a pint in one sitting and often do in the summer. If I'm eating a blueberry muffin, it had better be loaded, and this muffin definitely is! My secret to the softest muffin ever is the cake flour. It's actually a bit of a mystery muffin . . . totally tender yet dense and flavorful. You'll need to slow down on your first bite and really savor it. And then savor at least two more muffins because we're humans and we need to start the day off right.

PREP TIME: 15 minutes • **COOK TIME:** 27 to 30 minutes • **MAKES 15 MUFFINS**

1. Preheat the oven to 325°F. Line two muffin tins with fifteen cupcake liners.

2. **MAKE THE MUFFINS:** In the bowl of a stand mixer fitted with the paddle attachment or in a large bowl using a handheld mixer, combine the cream cheese and butter on medium-low speed until smooth, about 3 minutes. Gradually add the sugar and beat until the mixture is lighter and fluffier, 1 to 2 minutes. Add the eggs, one at a time, beating well after each addition. Add the vanilla. Add the flour all at once and mix until just combined. Reduce the speed to low, pour in the buttermilk, and mix until just incorporated.

3. Remove the bowl from the mixer and scrape down its sides with a rubber spatula. Use the spatula to gently fold in the blueberries.

4. **MAKE THE CRUMB TOPPING:** Using a food processor or in a medium bowl with a fork or your hands, combine the cubed cold butter, flour, and confectioners' sugar. Break down the butter into pieces no larger than the size of a pea.

5. **ASSEMBLE THE MUFFINS:** Add 2 or 3 tablespoons of batter to each lined muffin well; they will be about two-thirds full. Divide the crumb topping among the muffins.

6. Bake for 27 to 30 minutes. The muffins are done when a toothpick inserted into the center comes out with a few crumbs but no wet batter clinging to it.

7. Let the muffins cool for 5 minutes before serving.

8. Leftovers can be stored in an airtight container at room temperature for 1 or 2 days or in the refrigerator for up to 1 week.

MUFFINS

4 ounces (114 g) cream cheese, at room temperature

¾ cup (1½ sticks / 170 g) salted butter, at room temperature

1½ cups (300 g) granulated sugar

3 large eggs, at room temperature

1 teaspoon vanilla extract

1½ cups (192 g) cake flour

⅛ cup (30 ml) buttermilk, at room temperature

1 cup (148 g) fresh blueberries

CRUMB TOPPING

½ cup (1 stick / 113 g) cold unsalted butter, cubed

¾ cup (94 g) all-purpose flour

⅓ cup (42 g) confectioners' sugar

BANANA BANANA MUFFINS

Not a misprint, it really is banana banana. Actually, it is banana banana banana because I add more on top! I'm not known for my subtlety. You don't have to add the extra bananas on top, but if you like banana muffins as much as I do, it's worth trying.

PREP TIME: 10 minutes • **COOK TIME:** 16 to 18 minutes • **MAKES 20 MUFFINS**

1. Preheat the oven to 350°F. Line two muffin tins with twenty cupcake liners.

2. In a large bowl, mash 4 of the bananas. Add the butter, sugar, egg, and vanilla and mix well. Add the flour, baking soda, baking powder, and salt and mix until just incorporated.

3. Add 2 or 3 tablespoons of batter to each lined muffin well; they will be about two-thirds full. Top each with 3 slices from the remaining 2 bananas.

4. Bake for 16 to 18 minutes, until the centers of the muffins spring back when touched and no longer appear wet. Be careful to not bake the muffins for too long—you do not want burnt edges.

5. Let the muffins cool for about 5 minutes before serving.

6. Leftovers can be stored in an airtight container at room temperature for 1 or 2 days. The banana slices on top will brown, so they are best consumed immediately.

6 large ripe bananas

⅓ cup (71 g) unsalted butter, melted and slightly cooled

¾ cup (150 g) granulated sugar

1 large egg, at room temperature

1 teaspoon vanilla extract

1½ cups (188 g) all-purpose flour

1 teaspoon baking soda

1 teaspoon baking powder

½ teaspoon kosher salt

PULLED PORK HASH

This is my husband's culinary baby. He grew up with an amazing mother who not only taught him to cook but also inspired him to use his imagination and ingenuity in the kitchen. I hope I follow in her footsteps with my boys. But I digress. Chad whipped this up one morning and the entire family was in awe. He made it at least a dozen more times before we ever actually got a recipe written down, as it always seemed to change based on what was in the fridge. Be sure to try my Oven Pulled Pork (page 151) if you want some pretty serious flavor!

PREP TIME: 20 minutes • **COOK TIME:** 35 minutes • **MAKES 12 SERVINGS**

1. In a 15-inch skillet or large pot, heat 3 tablespoons of the oil over medium-high heat. Add the onions, bell peppers, and jalapeño and sauté until soft, 5 to 8 minutes. Add the garlic and cook for about 1 minute, until fragrant. Reduce the heat to medium. Add the pulled pork, paprika, 1 teaspoon salt, 1 teaspoon pepper, and 3 tablespoons of the remaining oil. Add the hash browns and fry for 25 minutes, or until crispy, stirring every few minutes.

2. Meanwhile, make the scrambled eggs. In a medium bowl, vigorously whisk the eggs and milk. In a medium skillet, heat up the remaining 1 tablespoon olive oil over medium heat. Add the egg mixture and let cook undisturbed for a few seconds to let the bottom of the eggs set. Drag a spatula down the middle of the eggs to expose the bottom of the skillet and let the uncooked eggs run into the exposed surface. Continue in this manner until the eggs are mostly cooked through. Remove from the heat.

3. Add 1 cup of the cheese to the pulled pork mixture and stir to combine. Add the scrambled eggs and stir to combine. Sprinkle the remaining ½ cup cheese on top. Season to taste with more salt and pepper and garnish with a few sliced jalapeños.

4. Serve hot.

5. Leftovers can be stored in an airtight container in the refrigerator for 1 or 2 days.

7 tablespoons olive oil

1 small yellow onion, finely diced (about ½ cup / 74 g)

1 small red onion, finely diced (about ½ cup / 74 g)

½ yellow bell pepper, seeded and finely diced (about ½ cup / 74 g)

½ red bell pepper, seeded and finely diced (about ½ cup / 74 g)

½ orange bell pepper, seeded and finely diced (about ½ cup / 74 g)

1 to 2 jalapeño peppers, seeded and finely diced (about ⅓ cup / 30 g; leave the seeds in for more heat), plus sliced jalapeños for garnish

2 tablespoons minced garlic

4 cups (1,000 g) Oven Pulled Pork (page 151)

1 tablespoon smoked paprika

Kosher salt

Freshly ground black pepper

One 32-ounce (908 g) bag frozen Southern-style hash browns

6 large eggs

½ cup (120 ml) whole milk

1½ cups (170 g) shredded Colby Jack or cheese of your choice

HOMEMADE SAUSAGE PATTIES WITH JALAPEÑO AND CHEDDAR

I really should have just written a book on breakfasts. In my humble opinion, there's nothing better than starting the day with a hot breakfast loaded with flavor. These sausage patties are so stinkin' fantastic—perfect with some eggs, a cup of freshly brewed coffee, and twelve-grain toast. This is the breakfast that makes me feel like a homesteader, like I'm fueling up for a tough day working the land. I mean, I don't actually do that, but I could after this breakfast.

PREP TIME: 20 minutes • **COOK TIME:** 10 minutes • **MAKES 14 PATTIES, ABOUT 7 SERVINGS**

1. In a large bowl, combine the ground sausage, onion, jalapeños, brown sugar, garlic, salt, black pepper, sage, garlic powder, marjoram, red pepper flakes, eggs, flour, cheese, and oil. Mix well.

2. Lay out a large piece of parchment paper on a work surface and spread half of the sausage mixture on top. Lay a matching piece of parchment paper over it. With a rolling pin, roll out the mixture to a thickness of about ½ inch. Remove the top layer of parchment paper. Press a cup or round 3½- to 4-inch cookie cutter into the mixture to form patties. Repeat to roll out the remaining sausage mixture. You will have enough for about 14 patties.

3. In a large skillet over medium-low heat, and working in batches as needed, cook the sausage patties for 4 to 5 minutes on each side, until browned and the internal temperature is 160°F.

4. Serve immediately.

5. Leftovers can be stored in an airtight container in the refrigerator for 2 or 3 days. To freeze, place the cooked patties on a baking sheet lined with parchment paper and freeze them for 30 minutes. Remove and transfer the patties to a freezer-safe bag or container. They will keep in the freezer for up to 3 months.

1 pound (454 g) ground pork sausage

1 small yellow onion, finely diced (about ½ cup / 74 g)

3 jalapeño peppers, seeded and finely diced (about ½ cup / 46 g; leave the seeds in for more heat)

1 tablespoon light brown sugar

1 teaspoon minced garlic

2 teaspoons kosher salt

1 teaspoon freshly ground black pepper

1 teaspoon dried sage

1 teaspoon garlic powder

¼ teaspoon dried marjoram

¼ teaspoon crushed red pepper flakes

2 large eggs

1 cup (125 g) all-purpose flour

1 cup (113 g) shredded sharp cheddar cheese

2 tablespoons olive oil

SAUSAGE, EGG, AND CHEESE BREAKFAST SLIDERS

Don't glance down quite yet . . . you might see that long ingredient list and dismiss these sliders. But just wait—let me tell you about them. The softest roll ever is paired with perfectly scrambled eggs, perfectly seasoned sausage, and a seasoned butter that will have you licking your fingers in delight. It all comes together pretty quickly, and you'll be left wondering, Where have these been all my life?

PREP TIME: 25 minutes • **COOK TIME:** 30 minutes • **MAKES 12 SLIDERS, ABOUT 6 SERVINGS**

SAUSAGE

2 tablespoons oil

1 pound (454 g) ground pork sausage

½ tablespoon light brown sugar

1 teaspoon kosher salt

½ teaspoon freshly ground black pepper

½ teaspoon dried sage

⅛ teaspoon dried marjoram

⅛ teaspoon crushed red pepper flakes

Pinch of ground cloves

EGGS

6 large eggs

½ teaspoon kosher salt

½ teaspoon freshly ground black pepper

1 teaspoon unsalted butter

SEASONED BUTTER

¼ cup (½ stick / 57 g) unsalted butter

¼ teaspoon onion salt

¼ teaspoon garlic salt

¼ teaspoon dried parsley

1. Preheat the oven to 350°F.

2. **COOK THE SAUSAGE:** In a large skillet over medium heat, heat the oil. Add the ground sausage, brown sugar, salt, pepper, sage, marjoram, red pepper flakes, and cloves. Mix well and cook until the sausage has browned, or until the internal temperature of the pork is 160°F, about 8 minutes.

3. **COOK THE EGGS:** In a medium bowl, vigorously whisk the eggs, salt, and pepper.

4. In a medium nonstick skillet over medium-low heat, heat the butter until just melted, swirling to coat the pan's surface. Add the eggs and cook undisturbed for a few seconds to let the bottom of the eggs set. Drag a spatula down the middle of the eggs to expose the bottom of the skillet and let the uncooked eggs run into the exposed surface. Continue in this manner until the eggs are mostly cooked through.

5. **MAKE THE SEASONED BUTTER:** In a small bowl, melt the butter in the microwave for a few seconds. Add the onion salt, garlic salt, and dried parsley and mix well. Set aside.

6. **ASSEMBLE THE SLIDERS:** Grease a 9 × 13-inch baking dish with nonstick spray.

7. Using a serrated knife, split all the Hawaiian rolls in half horizontally, placing the bottom halves in the prepared baking dish. Set the top halves aside. Lay the cheddar cheese, then the cooked sausage over the buns. Spread the eggs over the sausage, then lay the provolone slices on top. Add the top halves of the buns and brush them generously with the seasoned butter. Cover the pan with foil.

8. Bake for 20 minutes. Remove the foil and bake for 5 minutes more, or until the tops of the sliders are golden brown.

9. Slice and serve warm.

10. Store leftover sliders in an airtight container in the refrigerator for 1 or 2 days. To reheat, wrap a slider in a paper towel and heat in the microwave for 20 to 30 seconds, until warm throughout.

Nonstick spray

One 12-count package King's Hawaiian slider buns

6 slices cheddar cheese

6 slices provolone cheese

BREAKFAST PIE SKILLET

I found this recipe in a cookbook that my mother-in-law had saved from a church rummage sale. She loves rummage sales, and I love old church cookbooks. There's just something about a sparse ingredient list, less-than-detailed instructions, and seeing "Mrs. Gladys Nelson" scribbled underneath. I tested and tested (and tested, you're welcome) to get the right amounts of everything, and I think this breakfast pie is pretty darn fantastic.

PREP TIME: 15 minutes • **COOK TIME:** 25 minutes • **MAKES 6 SERVINGS**

1. Preheat the oven to 400°F.

2. In a 10-inch oven-safe skillet over medium heat, add the ground sausage and onion and cook until the sausage has browned or the internal temperature of the pork is 160°F, 8 to 10 minutes. Remove the skillet from the heat and drain. Sprinkle the cheese over the sausage and onion.

3. In a medium bowl, whisk the eggs, milk, half-and-half, Bisquick, ground mustard, salt, and pepper. Pour the egg mixture over the sausage.

4. Bake for 25 minutes, or until golden brown.

5. Serve hot.

6. To store leftovers, remove from the skillet and place in an airtight container in the refrigerator for 1 or 2 days.

1 pound (454 g) ground pork sausage

1 small white onion, finely diced (about ½ cup / 74 g)

1 cup (113 g) shredded cheddar cheese

4 large eggs

½ cup (120 ml) whole milk

½ cup (120 ml) half-and-half

2 cups (240 g) Bisquick pancake and baking mix

2 teaspoons ground mustard

½ teaspoon kosher salt

½ teaspoon freshly ground black pepper

APPETIZERS

AN APPETIZER IS defined as "a small dish of food or a drink taken before a meal or the main course of a meal to stimulate one's appetite." Weird right? Who considers drinks an appetizer? Not me. (I do include a Minnesota Martini in this chapter, but that is more of a fun treat than a recipe.)

For the purposes of this book, I would like to propose redefining an appetizer as "a dish of food consumed around a kitchen island or in front of a television that is meant to be accompanied by other appetizers, which are then consumed concurrently among several persons." Are you with me?!

Should *Webster's* choose to disregard my helpful suggestions, this is how the appetizers in this book are meant to be enjoyed.

Friends, family, a good game on the TV, and lots and lots of appetizers.

BACON-STUFFED MUSHROOMS

Let me be fully transparent here. I've never tried these. I have no idea how they taste. But I've made them several thousand times, and almost every time I make them for guests, someone asks for the recipe. They're a favorite of my husband, and I love making things that are just for him. He assures me that these are the best bacon-stuffed mushrooms he's ever had, and he's a good old midwestern boy, so you know he never tells tall tales.

PREP TIME: 20 minutes • **COOK TIME:** 30 minutes • **MAKES ABOUT 10 SERVINGS**

1. Preheat the oven to 350°F.

2. Clean the mushrooms with a damp paper towel. Carefully break off the stems and discard the tough ends. Finely chop the stems.

3. In a large oven-safe skillet over medium heat, heat the oil. Add the garlic, bell pepper, and chopped mushroom stems to the skillet. Sauté until any moisture has disappeared, 5 to 10 minutes, stirring frequently and taking care not to burn the garlic. Set aside to cool slightly, about 5 minutes.

4. Add the cream cheese, bacon, Asiago, pepper, onion powder, and cayenne to the skillet and stir to combine.

5. Fill each mushroom cap with a generous amount of the stuffing. To make this process easier, place the stuffing in a piping bag with the tip cut off (or a quart-size resealable plastic bag with a corner cut off) and squeeze the stuffing into the mushroom caps.

6. Arrange the mushroom caps on a large, clean oven-safe skillet and sprinkle them with the mozzarella.

7. Bake for 20 minutes, or until the mushrooms are piping hot and liquid starts to form under the caps.

8. Serve immediately.

9. Store leftover mushrooms in an airtight container in the refrigerator for 1 or 2 days. To reheat, wrap the mushrooms in paper towels and heat them in 15-second intervals in the microwave until warmed throughout.

1 pound (454 g) whole baby bella mushrooms

1 tablespoon extra-virgin olive oil

1 tablespoon minced garlic

¼ red bell pepper, seeded and diced (about ¼ cup / 37 g)

One 8-ounce (227 g) package cream cheese, at room temperature

8 to 10 bacon slices, cooked until crisp, then crumbled (about 1½ cups / 149 g)

¼ cup (25 g) grated Asiago cheese

¼ teaspoon freshly ground black pepper

¼ teaspoon onion powder

¼ teaspoon cayenne pepper

¼ cup (28 g) shredded mozzarella cheese

JALAPEÑO POPPERS

The ingredients in these jalapeño poppers are pretty standard, but I tweaked the method a bit. Whenever I made them the traditional way, with the bacon wrapped around, the bacon on the bottom was always soggy and chewy, which I thought took away from the overall texture. In this version I bake the bacon separately and add it on top of the jalapeño poppers. This means crispy bacon, creamy cream cheese, and jalapeño. Appetizer awesomeness.

PREP TIME: 20 minutes • **COOK TIME:** 30 minutes • **MAKES 20 POPPERS, ABOUT 10 SERVINGS**

1. Preheat the oven to 425°F. Line a sheet pan with foil or parchment paper.

2. Arrange the bacon on the prepared sheet pan. Bake for 10 minutes, or to your desired doneness. (The slices will crisp up on top of the jalapeños, so I tend to underbake.) Break each piece of bacon in half.

3. In a large bowl, mix together the cream cheese, Parmesan, onion powder, and pepper until combined. Spoon about 1 tablespoon of the mixture into each jalapeño half. Arrange the stuffed halves on a sheet pan (I like to line mine with foil). Sprinkle cheddar cheese on top of the cream cheese mixture. Place a piece of bacon on top of each popper and press down slightly.

4. Bake for 20 minutes, or until bubbly and lightly browned.

5. Serve immediately.

6. Leftovers can be stored in an airtight container in the refrigerator for 1 or 2 days.

5 bacon slices, halved crosswise (about ⅔ cup / 76 g)

One 8-ounce (227 g) package cream cheese, at room temperature

1 cup (100 g) grated Parmesan cheese

¼ teaspoon onion powder

¼ teaspoon freshly ground black pepper

10 large jalapeño peppers (200 g), halved lengthwise and seeded

1 cup (113 g) shredded cheddar cheese

MIDWESTERN SMOKIES

Bacon-wrapped smokies with CREAM CHEESE! I feel shouting is appropriate because it adds something amazing to these well-known treats. Not only does the cream cheese contribute a smooth, cooling element to the smokies, but the sauce! It's perfect with these smokies. You may want to make a double batch of the dip, because it makes everything taste better.

PREP TIME: 20 minutes • **COOK TIME:** 30 minutes • **MAKES 8 SERVINGS**

1. Preheat the oven to 425°F. Line a sheet pan with parchment paper and arrange the bacon on the prepared pan.

2. Combine the brown sugar, chili powder, paprika, garlic powder, onion powder, jalapeño powder, and cayenne in a medium bowl. Sprinkle half the smokies seasoning over the bacon.

3. Bake for 10 minutes and remove from the oven. (The bacon will not be crispy.)

4. Reduce the oven temperature to 325°F.

5. As soon as the bacon is cool to the touch, spread about ½ teaspoon of cream cheese on each piece. Roll up a smokie in each bacon half and secure with a toothpick. Set the smokies on the sheet pan as you finish. Sprinkle the remaining smokies seasoning on top and bake for 15 to 20 minutes, until the bacon is crispy.

6. Serve warm with the dipping sauce.

7. Leftovers can be stored in an airtight container in the refrigerator for 1 or 2 days.

1½ pounds (681 g) bacon (not thick cut), halved crosswise

1 cup (200 g) packed light brown sugar

1 tablespoon chili powder

1 teaspoon paprika

1 teaspoon garlic powder

1 teaspoon onion powder

1 teaspoon jalapeño powder

¼ teaspoon cayenne pepper

4 ounces (114 g) cream cheese, at room temperature

One 14-ounce (397 g) package cocktail smokies

Dipping Sauce (optional; recipe follows)

Dipping Sauce

PREP TIME: 5 minutes • **MAKES ½ CUP**

In a medium bowl, combine the sour cream, ketchup, brown sugar, hot sauce, jalapeño powder, and chives. Set in the refrigerator to chill until ready to use.

¼ cup (58 g) sour cream

¼ cup (60 g) ketchup

1 tablespoon light brown sugar

1 tablespoon hot sauce

½ teaspoon jalapeño powder

½ teaspoon minced fresh chives

EIGHT-LAYER DIP

Most folks have heard of and love seven-layer dip. For good reason. It is a fabulous combination of all the things we want in a dip! But I added a layer that most midwestern folks will love. Corn. And not just any corn, *roasted* corn. Roasting the corn provides a subtle sweetness to this super-savory dish. I love to serve this messy since it gets devoured in three seconds flat anyway.

PREP TIME: 20 minutes • **COOK TIME:** 10 to 15 minutes • **MAKES 12 SERVINGS**

1. In a large skillet, heat the oil over medium heat.

2. Add the corn and cook, stirring often, for about 10 minutes, until the corn starts to brown. (You can also roast the corn in a 400°F oven on a sheet pan for 10 to 15 minutes.) Set the corn aside in the skillet.

3. In a medium bowl, combine the tomatoes, onion, jalapeño, and cilantro. Add the juice of 1 lime and the salt. Stir to combine and set aside.

4. In a separate medium bowl, combine the avocados and half the tomato mixture. (Reserve the other half for another layer.)

5. Spread the refried beans onto a large serving platter in a flat, smooth layer. (A small offset spatula works great here.) Add dollops of the sour cream on top and carefully spread in an even layer over the refried beans. Spoon dollops of the tomato and avocado mixture over the sour cream and spread in an even layer. Sprinkle the olives, then the cheeses on top. Add the remaining tomato mixture, followed by the roasted corn. Squeeze juice from the remaining lime on top, adding as much or as little as you would like.

6. Serve with tortilla chips for scooping.

NOTE: Add cooked ground beef or shredded rotisserie chicken for an extra layer.

1 tablespoon vegetable oil

One 15.25-ounce (432 g) can corn kernels, drained

6 Roma tomatoes, finely diced (about 3 cups / 600 g)

1 small white onion, finely diced (about ½ cup / 74 g)

1 large jalapeño pepper, seeded and diced (about ¼ cup / 23 g; leave the seeds in for more heat)

¼ cup (4 g) finely chopped fresh cilantro, or to taste

2 limes

Pinch of kosher salt

2 large ripe Haas avocados, halved, pitted, peeled, and finely diced

One 16-ounce (454 g) can refried beans

1 cup (230 g) sour cream

½ cup (90 g) sliced black olives

¾ cup (85 g) grated Monterey Jack cheese

¾ cup (85 g) grated cheddar cheese

Tortilla chips, for serving

BACON CORN DIP

I started serving this for our small-group Bible study years ago. Even the folks who didn't like certain ingredients seemed to love this dip. I love prepping this dish for some reason. Chopping the onions and shredding the cheese is all very calming. Then, because I am a good host, I am required to taste-test before serving, and that first bite—well. It's heavenly. Please note that this does make a large amount. I use a 12-inch skillet and it's full! You can easily halve this recipe.

PREP TIME: 20 minutes • **COOK TIME:** 40 to 50 minutes • **MAKES 16 SERVINGS**

1. Preheat the oven to 350°F.

2. In a large bowl, combine the corn, cream cheese, cheddar, mozzarella, Parmesan, and jalapeños (reserving some diced jalapeños for garnish, if desired). Stir with a spatula until combined. Mix in the crumbled bacon (reserving some for garnish, if desired) and the onions. Season with the salt and pepper.

3. Pour the mixture into a large oven-safe skillet. Bake, uncovered, for 40 to 50 minutes, until the cheese is melted, hot, and bubbly.

4. Garnish with the reserved jalapeños and bacon. Serve warm, right out of the skillet, with crackers.

5. Leftovers can be stored in an airtight container in the refrigerator for 1 or 2 days.

Four 15.25-ounce (1.7 kg total) cans corn kernels, drained

Two 8-ounce (454 g total) packages cream cheese, at room temperature

2 cups (226 g) shredded cheddar cheese

2 cups (226 g) shredded mozzarella cheese

1 cup (100 g) grated Parmesan cheese

2 jalapeño peppers, finely diced (about 1/3 cup / 30 g)

1½ pounds (15 slices) thick-cut bacon, cooked until crisp, then crumbled (about 2 cups / 224 g)

2 small red onions, finely diced (about 1 cup / 148 g)

1 teaspoon kosher salt

½ teaspoon freshly ground black pepper

Crackers, for serving

AIR FRYER MAPLE-MUSTARD PORK BELLY BITES

The air fryer, oh how I love thee. Since writing this book, I have designated a new spot on my counter for the air fryer. It makes everything better, and I do mean everything. I know this to be a fact because my husband smokes the best pork belly bite ever. We entice people to our home on the promise of his smoked meat prowess. But then one cold Minnesota day, I had a craving and popped some pork belly bites in the air fryer. I was changed. They were done in twenty-five minutes and tasted even better than when smoked. Imagine my shock and delight! This is one of those must-try recipes . . . and that maple mustard sauce is going to change your life for the better.

PREP TIME: 30 minutes • **COOK TIME:** 22 to 25 minutes • **MAKES 45 BITES, ABOUT 9 SERVINGS**

1. Preheat the air fryer to 400°F.

2. Pat the pork belly dry with paper towels and cut it into 1-inch pieces. (If the pork belly has warmed to room temperature, put it in the refrigerator for a few minutes to firm it up a bit for easier cutting.)

3. In a large bowl, combine the oil, salt, and pepper. Add the pork belly pieces and toss to cover each piece.

4. Working in batches, lay the pork belly pieces in a single layer in the air fryer basket. Air-fry the pork belly cubes for 22 to 25 minutes, shaking and flipping them a couple of times during the cooking time. (Note: Air-frying times will depend on the size of your pork belly pieces and the size of your air fryer.) Remove the bites from the air fryer, place in a large bowl, and tent with foil to keep warm. Repeat to cook the remaining pork belly bites.

5. Meanwhile, in a small bowl, mix together the maple syrup, mustard, and vinegar. Set aside 3 tablespoons of the syrup mixture for dipping.

6. Pour the rest of the syrup mixture all over the bites and toss to coat.

7. Serve warm with the reserved dipping sauce.

3 pounds (1.4 kg) pork belly

6 tablespoons canola oil

2 teaspoons kosher salt

2 teaspoons freshly ground black pepper

½ cup (120 ml) pure maple syrup

3 tablespoons Dijon mustard

3 teaspoons apple cider vinegar

MINNESOTA MARTINI

This drink, whose official name is Beertini, is simply a light beer (usually Michelob Golden Light, but I prefer Miller Lite) with green olives. While other states lay claim to it (there is a North Dakota Martini and a Wisconsin Martini), mine will always be a Minnesota Martini. It's very much a midwestern thing.

I've yet to hear an official story of origin for a Beertini, but the myth is that farmers wanted a fresh cold beer and a snack and, being as time efficient as they are, added the green olives to the beer and called it a day. Beer enthusiasts don't recommend adding olives to a beer with a solid flavor profile, like an IPA, because it will alter the flavor of craft brews. I would definitely consider myself a beer enthusiast who just so happens to be enthusiastic about only one beer, and that beer is Miller Lite.

As an added bonus, you get a snack at the end of your drink!

PREP TIME: 2 minutes • **MAKES 1 SERVING**

Pour the beer into a frosty mug and top with the olives. Enjoy!

One 12-ounce (360 ml) light beer

3 pimento-stuffed green olives

DILL PICKLE CHEESE BALL BITES

Cheese balls were the mysterious glob of something-or-other served at parties and on holidays when I was a kid. I didn't really understand them and for a long time wasn't brave enough to try one. But eventually I did—and I was hooked. But when it came to making them myself, I wanted something easier—more single-serving friendly. So these mini cheese ball bites were born. In addition to the ease of serving, you get the crispy coating around every single bite!

PREP TIME: 15 minutes • **CHILLING TIME:** 1 hour • **MAKES 16 CHEESE BITES, ABOUT 4 SERVINGS**

1. Line a sheet pan with a piece of parchment paper.

2. In a medium bowl, mix together the cream cheese, diced pickles, ham, and ranch seasoning until combined. Form the cream cheese mixture into 16 small balls (about ½ inch in diameter). Place each cheese ball onto the prepared sheet pan.

3. Refrigerate the cheese balls for about 1 hour, until firm.

4. Meanwhile, in a small bowl or on a plate, stir together the chives, pecans, and minced pickles.

5. Roll the cheese balls into the coating mixture. If not serving immediately, loosely cover the cheese bites with plastic wrap and store in the refrigerator. Let them come to room temperature for 15 minutes before serving.

One 8-ounce (227 g) package cream cheese, at room temperature

½ cup (72 g) finely diced dill pickles, plus 1/2 cup (48 g) finely minced

½ cup (68 g) finely diced deli ham

3 tablespoons Homemade Ranch Seasoning Mix (page 157)

⅓ cup (15 g) finely minced fresh chives

⅓ cup (36 g) finely chopped pecans

MINNESOTA CAVIAR

This is the appetizer known as cowboy caviar, but with a super-special ingredient: zucchini. You'll hear a lot about my love of zucchini in this book, but that love has stemmed from need. Zucchini grows so fast, and "waste not, want not," so I put it in everything, and it just so happens that zucchini adds something to traditional cowboy caviar that I love. You don't have to peel it—I rarely do—but I was trying to make it pretty, just for you.

PREP TIME: 15 minutes • **MAKES 12 SERVINGS**

2 small zucchini, peeled or unpeeled, finely chopped (about 4 cups / 430 g)

1 red bell pepper, seeded and finely diced (about 1 cup / 150 g)

1 orange bell pepper, seeded and finely diced (about 1 cup / 150 g)

1 yellow bell pepper, seeded and finely diced (about 1 cup / 150 g)

1 small red onion, finely chopped (about 1 cup / 136 g)

1 jalapeño pepper, seeded and minced (about ¼ cup / 32 g; leave the seeds in for more heat)

10 ounces cherry tomatoes, diced (1½ cups / 283 g)

One 15.25-ounce (432 g) can yellow corn kernels, drained

One 11-ounce (312 g) can white corn kernels, drained

One 15-ounce (425 g) can black beans, rinsed and drained

1 tablespoon finely chopped fresh cilantro

1 cup (231 g) Italian vinaigrette dressing, or less to taste

In a large bowl, combine the zucchini, bell peppers, onion, jalapeño, cherry tomatoes, yellow and white corn, black beans, and cilantro. Pour up to 1 cup of the Italian vinaigrette dressing over the vegetables, starting with less and tasting to see if more is needed. Mix well, adjust the dressing as desired, and serve.

MUSHROOM SWISS SLIDERS

Raise your hand if you don't like mushrooms. (I'm raising my hand.) But that didn't stop me from trying these mushroom sliders several years ago and realizing that I *love* them. Something about the bread, the meat and cheese, and that perfectly seasoned butter rocked my world. So while you'll never see mushroom risotto near me, you will see me sneak a few of these into my office so I can eat them in glorious peace. Because they are that good.

See the photo on page 54.

PREP TIME: 25 minutes • **COOK TIME:** 45 minutes • **MAKES 12 SLIDERS, ABOUT 6 SERVINGS**

Nonstick spray

HAMBURGER

1 tablespoon seasoned salt

1 tablespoon Hamburger Seasoning Mix (page 157)

¼ teaspoon kosher salt

¼ teaspoon freshly ground black pepper

1 tablespoon canola oil

½ small yellow onion, diced (about ½ cup / 74 g)

1 teaspoon minced garlic

1 pound (454 g) ground beef

½ teaspoon Worcestershire sauce

MUSHROOM SWISS SAUCE

½ cup (1 stick / 114 g) unsalted butter

8 ounces (227 g) baby bella mushrooms, sliced (about 1 cup)

¼ cup (60 ml) beef broth

¼ cup (60 ml) whole milk

½ cup (57 g) shredded Swiss cheese

1. Preheat the oven to 350°F. Grease a 9 × 13-inch baking dish with nonstick spray.

2. **MAKE THE HAMBURGER:** In a small bowl, mix together the seasoned salt, hamburger seasoning, salt, and pepper. Set aside.

3. In a large nonstick skillet over medium heat, heat the oil. Add the onion and garlic and sauté until fragrant, 1 to 2 minutes. Add the ground beef to the pan. Break up the meat with a wooden spoon. Add the Worcestershire sauce and sprinkle the beef with the seasoning mixture. Cook for 8 to 10 minutes, stirring occasionally, until no pink remains in the meat. Remove the skillet from the heat and drain.

4. **MAKE THE MUSHROOM SWISS SAUCE:** In a medium saucepan over medium heat, melt the butter. Add the mushrooms and cook for 5 to 10 minutes, until the mushrooms are softened. Add the broth and milk. Reduce the heat to low and slowly add the cheese, whisking constantly until the cheese is completely melted. Add the cooked hamburger and stir to combine. Set aside.

5. **MAKE THE SEASONED BUTTER:** In a small bowl, mix the melted butter, garlic salt, sesame seeds, and parsley. Set aside.

6. **BAKE THE SLIDERS:** Using a serrated knife, split all the Hawaiian rolls in half horizontally. Place the bottom halves in the prepared baking dish. Lay 6 slices of the cheese over the rolls, followed by the hamburger mixture, then the remaining 6 cheese slices. Place the top halves of the buns on top and brush the tops with the seasoned butter.

7. Cover the dish with foil and bake for 20 minutes, or until the cheese is hot and bubbly. Remove the foil and bake for 5 minutes more, or until the tops of the sliders are golden brown.

8. Cut individual rolls and serve hot.

9. Store leftover sliders in an airtight container in the refrigerator for 1 or 2 days. To reheat, wrap a slider in a paper towel and heat in the microwave for 20 to 30 seconds, until warm throughout.

SEASONED BUTTER

¼ cup (½ stick / 57 g) unsalted butter, melted

1 teaspoon garlic salt

2 teaspoons sesame seeds

1 teaspoon dried parsley

SLIDERS

One 12-count package King's Hawaiian slider buns

12 deli slices Swiss cheese

MUSHROOM SWISS SLIDERS, PAGE 52

CHEESEBURGER SLIDERS, PAGE 56

CHEESEBURGER SLIDERS

Sliders are a gift to moms everywhere. A complete meal in one pan! As a mom of five precious kiddos, I often make two pans. I like to really season the meat so that it tastes just like a grilled hamburger (arguably my favorite food on the planet).

See the photo on page 55.

PREP TIME: 20 minutes • **COOK TIME:** 30 minutes • **MAKES 12 SLIDERS, ABOUT 6 SERVINGS**

Nonstick spray

HAMBURGER

½ teaspoon Lawry's Seasoned Salt

1 tablespoon Hamburger Seasoning Mix (page 157)

¼ teaspoon kosher salt

¼ teaspoon freshly ground black pepper

1 tablespoon canola oil

1 small yellow onion, finely chopped (about ½ cup / 74 g)

1 garlic clove, minced

1 pound (454 g) ground beef

½ teaspoon Worcestershire sauce

SEASONED BUTTER

¼ cup (½ stick / 57 g) unsalted butter, melted

½ teaspoon kosher salt

½ teaspoon freshly coarse-ground black pepper

2 teaspoons sesame seeds

SLIDERS

One 12-count package King's Hawaiian slider buns

12 deli slices cheddar cheese

1 cup (143 g) diced dill pickles

1 medium tomato, finely diced (about 1 cup / 180 g)

1 cup (113 g) shredded cheddar cheese

1. Preheat the oven to 350°F. Grease a 9 × 13-inch baking dish with nonstick spray.

2. **MAKE THE HAMBURGER:** In a small bowl, mix the seasoned salt, hamburger seasoning, salt, and pepper. Set aside.

3. In a large nonstick skillet over medium heat, heat the oil. Add the onion and garlic and sauté until fragrant, 1 to 2 minutes. Add the ground beef and break up the meat with a wooden spoon. Add the Worcestershire sauce and sprinkle the beef with the seasoning mixture. Cook for 8 to 10 minutes, until no pink remains in the meat. Remove the skillet from the heat and drain.

4. **MAKE THE SEASONED BUTTER:** In a small bowl, mix the melted butter, salt, coarse-ground pepper, and sesame seeds. Set aside.

5. **BAKE THE SLIDERS:** Using a serrated knife, split all the Hawaiian rolls in half horizontally. Place the bottom halves of the rolls in the prepared dish. Lay the cheese slices on the bottom halves and top with the cooked hamburger. Sprinkle on the diced pickles, tomatoes, and shredded cheese. Place the top halves of the buns on top and brush the tops with the seasoned butter.

6. Cover the dish with foil and bake for 15 minutes, or until the cheese is hot and bubbly. Remove the foil and bake for 5 minutes more, or until the tops of the sliders are golden brown.

7. Cut individual rolls and serve hot.

8. Store leftover sliders in an airtight container in the refrigerator for 1 or 2 days. To reheat, wrap a slider in a paper towel and heat in the microwave for 20 to 30 seconds, until warm throughout.

CARAMELIZED ONION ROLLS WITH GARLICKY CREAM CHEESE FILLING

A wonderfully soft, sweet dough filled with perfectly caramelized onions on a bed of cream cheese. Because you make your own dough here, this side dish takes a bit of time, but it's well worth it.

PREP TIME: 40 minutes • **RESTING TIME:** 2 hours • **COOK TIME:** 50 minutes • **MAKES 12 ROLLS**

1. **MAKE THE DOUGH:** In a medium bowl, combine the milk and 1 tablespoon of the sugar. Sprinkle the yeast over the milk and whisk to blend. Let sit until the yeast is foamy, about 5 minutes. Add the eggs. Whisk until smooth.

2. In the bowl of a stand mixer fitted with the dough hook attachment, combine the remaining 4 tablespoons sugar, the flour, and salt. Add the milk mixture and combine. With the mixer running on medium speed, add the butter, one piece at a time, blending well between additions. Knead in the mixer for 1 minute.

3. Increase the mixer speed to medium-high and knead until the dough is soft, about 5 minutes. If the dough doesn't come together, add more flour, 1 tablespoon at a time.

4. Brush a medium bowl with some of the melted butter. Place the dough in the bowl and brush the top of the dough with the remaining melted butter. Cover with plastic wrap. Let the dough rise in a warm, draft-free area until doubled in size, about 1 hour. While the dough is rising, prepare the caramelized onions and cream cheese filling.

5. **MAKE THE CARAMELIZED ONIONS:** In a medium sauté pan, heat the butter and oil over medium heat. Add the onion. Cook, uncovered, stirring frequently, until sticky, about 10 minutes. Add the salt and sugar and cook for about 10 minutes more, stirring occasionally, until browned. Set aside to cool.

(continued)

DOUGH

⅔ cup (160 ml) whole milk, warmed in the microwave for about 30 seconds to 100°F

5 tablespoons granulated sugar

2 teaspoons active dry yeast

2 large eggs, at room temperature

2¾ cups (344 g) all-purpose flour, plus more as needed and for rolling out the dough

1 teaspoon kosher salt

½ cup (1 stick / 114 g) unsalted butter, cut into 1-inch chunks, at room temperature

½ tablespoon unsalted butter, melted

CARAMELIZED ONIONS

1 tablespoon unsalted butter

1 tablespoon vegetable oil

1 small red onion, finely diced (about ½ cup / 74 g)

½ teaspoon kosher salt

½ teaspoon granulated sugar

GARLICKY CREAM CHEESE FILLING

One 8-ounce (227 g) package cream cheese, at room temperature

2 teaspoons minced fresh chives

2 teaspoons minced garlic

½ teaspoon kosher salt

Nonstick spray

2 cups (226 g) shredded Gruyère cheese

BUTTER TOPPING

3 tablespoons unsalted butter, melted

1 teaspoon minced garlic

1 teaspoon minced fresh chives

1 teaspoon kosher salt

1 tablespoon grated Parmesan cheese

6. **MAKE THE GARLICKY CREAM CHEESE FILLING:** In a medium bowl, beat the cream cheese, chives, garlic, and salt until smooth.

7. **ASSEMBLE AND BAKE THE ROLLS:** Grease a 9 × 13-inch baking dish with nonstick spray.

8. When the dough is ready, punch the dough, turn it out onto a floured surface, and roll it into a 10 × 15-inch rectangle that's about ¼ inch thick.

9. Spread the cream cheese mixture over the dough. Top the mixture with the Gruyère and caramelized onions.

10. Roll up the dough tightly, starting on the long edge. Using a very sharp knife, cut the log into 12 rolls. Place them into the prepared baking dish. Let rise in a warm place until doubled in size, about 1 hour.

11. In the last 15 minutes of rise time, preheat the oven to 350°F.

12. Bake for 25 to 30 minutes. Set the rolls aside to cool in the pan for 5 minutes.

13. **MAKE THE BUTTER TOPPING:** In a small bowl, combine the melted butter, garlic, chives, and salt. Brush over the warm rolls and sprinkle with the Parmesan cheese.

14. Serve warm.

15. Leftovers can be stored in an airtight container in the refrigerator for 1 or 2 days.

SKILLET BEER CHEESE BREAD

This recipe combines two of my favorite things: skillet recipes and beer bread. The amount of butter in this dish is nothing short of ridiculous, and when you see it bubbling in the skillet, you just might doubt me. But wait a few minutes: Cut your first slice. Then take your first bite. I have a feeling you won't doubt me anymore.

PREP TIME: 10 minutes • **COOK TIME:** 35 to 45 minutes • **MAKES 12 SERVINGS**

1. Preheat the oven to 375°F. Grease a 12-inch oven-safe skillet with nonstick spray.

2. In a large bowl, whisk the flour, baking powder, and salt together well. Fold in 1 cup of the cheese. Pour in the beer and stir until the batter is just combined, with no dry parts (it will be thick). Pour the batter into the prepared skillet and smooth it out.

3. Cut the butter into 8 slices and place them evenly on top of the batter. Sprinkle with the remaining 1 cup cheese.

4. Bake for 35 to 45 minutes, until the bread is golden brown on top, with about ½ inch of melted butter bubbling at the bottom. Let cool on the counter for about 5 minutes, until the butter is soaked back up into the bread.

5. Serve warm, cut into wedges and garnished with diced green onion.

6. Leftovers can be stored covered at room temperature for 1 or 2 days.

Nonstick spray

3 cups (375 g) all-purpose flour

1 tablespoon baking powder

2 teaspoons kosher salt

2 cups (226 g) shredded cheddar cheese

One 12-ounce (360 ml) bottle of beer, at room temperature (I prefer light beer)

½ cup (1 stick / 114 g) cold salted or unsalted butter

1 tablespoon finely diced green onion, for garnish

ONION BACON JAM

If you've never made this jam before, this is your sign that it's time. I can't keep it in my fridge—it usually gets devoured the same day! We like it on crackers, bread, and burgers, over French fries and topped with cheese . . . the possibilities are endless.

PREP TIME: 20 minutes • **COOK TIME:** 45 minutes • **MAKES 2½ CUPS**

1. In a medium saucepan over medium heat, cook the bacon until crispy, about 15 minutes, depending on the size of the slices. Remove the bacon to a plate lined with paper towels to drain. When cool, break the bacon into 1-inch pieces. Set aside.

2. Drain the bacon fat, reserving about 4 tablespoons in the pan. (Be careful, it is hot!)

3. Add the onion and shallot to the pan over medium-low heat. Cook until the onion is sticky and browned, stirring often, 15 to 20 minutes. Mix in the garlic, brown sugar, vinegar, maple syrup, chili powder, and bacon. Simmer for 7 to 10 minutes, until the mixture has thickened to the consistency of jam.

4. Serve warm or cold, but you may want to warm it slightly if it has been refrigerated.

1 pound (454 g) bacon

1 large yellow onion, finely chopped (about 3 cups / 444 g)

2 large shallots, finely diced (about 1½ cups / 222 g)

2 garlic cloves, minced

½ cup (100 g) packed light brown sugar

⅓ cup (80 ml) apple cider vinegar

¼ cup (60 ml) pure maple syrup

1 teaspoon chili powder (optional but highly recommended)

SKILLET HAMBURGER NACHOS

If you told me I could use only cast-iron skillets for the rest of my life, I would be thrilled. To my mind, they just make everything better. For instance, nachos (and all their glorious cheese) stay warmer for longer. Even though this is a big serving, everything will taste amazing down to the last bite.

PREP TIME: 15 minutes • **COOK TIME:** 10 minutes • **MAKES 8 SERVINGS**

1. Preheat the oven to 425°F.

2. In a large saucepan over medium heat, add the onion and sauté until fragrant, 1 to 2 minutes. Add the ground beef and cook until the beef is no longer pink, about 8 minutes. Remove the saucepan from the heat and drain. Add the taco seasoning and refried beans to the saucepan. Mix well.

3. Add one third of the tortilla chips to a large oven-safe skillet. Top with one third of the beef-bean mixture, one third of the cheeses, and one third of the black beans. Repeat to make two more layers.

4. Bake until the cheese is melted, about 10 minutes.

5. Top with the diced tomato, green onion, cilantro, and jalapeños. Dollop with sour cream and serve.

1 small yellow onion, finely diced (about ½ cup / 74 g)

1 pound (454 g) ground beef

2 tablespoons (28 g) Homemade Taco Seasoning (page 156)

One 15-ounce (425 g) can refried beans

1 large bag tortilla chips (about 13 ounces)

2 cups (113 g) shredded mild cheddar cheese

2 cups (113 g) shredded Monterey Jack cheese

½ cup (86 g) canned black beans, drained and rinsed

1 large tomato, finely diced (about 1¼ cups / 250 g)

3 green onions, sliced (about ¼ cup / 25 g)

¼ cup chopped fresh cilantro

2 jalapeño peppers, seeded and diced (about ⅓ cup / 30 g; leave the seeds in for more heat)

Sour cream, for topping

ROASTED ASPARAGUS PUFF PASTRY

I am forever trying to come up with ways to wow dinner guests with minimal time and effort. When you're preparing three or four different dishes, saving time on one can be a sanity-saver. But you also want to impress! This is that dish. Buttery-rich puff pastry is complemented with asparagus, cheese, and Onion Bacon Jam (page 63). You could swap regular cooked bacon for the bacon jam if you really have to, but try it as is just once, pretty please.

PREP TIME: 10 minutes • **COOK TIME:** 20 to 22 minutes • **MAKES 6 SERVINGS**

1. Preheat the oven to 400°F. Line a sheet pan with parchment paper.

2. In a large skillet or sauté pan, bring 1 inch of water to a boil over medium heat. Add the asparagus and cook for 5 minutes, or until bright green. Drain the liquid from the skillet. Add the oil, salt, pepper, and garlic. Toss to coat.

3. Lay out the thawed puff pastry on the prepared sheet pan. Brush the pastry with the egg wash. Top the pastry with the cheese slices, leaving about a ½-inch border around the edges. Lay the asparagus on top in an even layer.

4. Bake for 20 to 22 minutes, until the pastry edges are puffy and golden brown.

5. Top with the onion bacon jam. Cut into strips and serve.

½ pound (227 g) asparagus, woody ends removed

1 tablespoon olive oil

½ teaspoon kosher salt

½ teaspoon freshly ground black pepper

3 garlic cloves, minced

1 sheet frozen puff pastry, thawed according to the package instructions

1 large egg, whisked, for an egg wash

8 ounces (227 g) fresh mozzarella cheese, cut into ¼-inch-thick slices

¼ cup Onion Bacon Jam (page 63)

BUFFALO ONION RINGS

Welcome to my brain! I had the crazy idea for this recipe, and let me tell you, testing it made for the best couple of weeks! Pairing onion rings with Buffalo sauce is a match made in heaven. Plus, I have to open a beer to make these, which means I have to drink some beer, and that is the trifecta of awesomeness.

PREP TIME: 40 minutes • **COOK TIME:** 2 to 4 minutes • **MAKES ABOUT 24 ONION RINGS**

1. Soak the onion slices in an ice bath for 30 minutes. This gives you a crispier onion ring. (For an even crispier onion ring, remove the inner membranes of the onion slices.) Pat the onions dry with paper towels.

2. Fill a large heavy-bottomed pot with at least 2 inches of oil. Heat the oil to 375°F to 400°F, using a thermometer to check the temperature.

3. In a large bowl, whisk the flour, baking powder, and salt. Add the egg, beer, and Buffalo sauce and whisk to combine. Add more beer if you prefer a thinner batter.

4. Dip 2 or 3 onion rings in the batter and drop them into the hot oil for 1 to 2 minutes per side, until golden. Using a slotted spoon, remove the onion rings from the oil and place on a plate lined with paper towels. Repeat with the remaining onion rings. The oil will cool down a bit with each batch, so be sure to check its temperature between batches. Cooler oil means less crispy onion rings.

5. Drizzle with the extra Buffalo sauce and serve hot with ranch dressing for dipping.

6. These are best eaten hot. If you do have leftovers, they can be stored in an airtight container at room temperature for 1 or 2 days.

2 or 3 large yellow onions (444 g), cut into ½-inch-thick rings

4 cups (960 ml) vegetable oil

1 cup (125 g) all-purpose flour

1½ teaspoons baking powder

½ teaspoon kosher salt

1 large egg, at room temperature

½ cup (118 g) light beer, such as Miller Lite or Michelob Golden Light, plus more if needed

1¼ cups (341 g) Frank's RedHot Buffalo sauce, plus more for drizzling

Ranch or blue cheese dressing, for dipping

PIGGY PICKLE PIZZA

Let me just tell you about this pizza. It's amazing, it's delicious, it's a fantastic mash-up of flavors that you're going to love. Here is the thing with this pizza—it's different. You want to savor each bite. There's no rushing! It's almost like a gourmet pizza in that you need only a slice or two. I know that sounds crazy and probably goes against every precious preconceived notion we have about how to consume pizza—but it's true. This is more like an *appetizer* pizza. I would cut it up and serve it with Air Fryer Maple-Mustard Pork Belly Bites (page 45), Buffalo Onion Rings (page 69), and even Cheeseburger Sliders (page 56). This could be the pizza you're *known* for—one that sparks conversation and always leaves smiles on people's faces.

PREP TIME: 65 minutes • **COOK TIME:** 20 minutes • **MAKES 8 SERVINGS**

ALFREDO SAUCE

Head of garlic (Do not use pre-peeled garlic.)

1 teaspoon olive oil

2 tablespoons salted butter

1 cup (240 ml) heavy cream

½ teaspoon kosher salt

⅛ teaspoon freshly ground black pepper

½ cup (50 g) freshly grated Parmesan cheese

1. Preheat the oven to 400°F. If using a pizza stone, place it in the cold oven to preheat.

2. **MAKE THE ALFREDO SAUCE:** Use your fingers to peel away all the loose, papery outer layers around the garlic head, leaving the head itself intact, with all the cloves connected. Cut off the top half of the garlic head, just enough to expose the cloves. Place the garlic head cut side up in the middle of a 6-inch foil square. Drizzle with the oil, letting the oil soak in around the cloves. Fold the foil up around the garlic to create a sealed packet.

3. Bake for about 55 minutes, until the garlic cloves are soft and deep golden brown.

4. Carefully open the sealed packet and set the garlic head aside to cool slightly. When cool to the touch, squeeze out the cloves onto a cutting board. Discard the remaining skin. Chop the roasted garlic and set aside.

5. Melt the butter in a large saucepan over medium heat. Add the cream, salt, and pepper and stir to combine. Bring the mixture to a slow rolling boil, stirring often. Reduce the heat to low and boil gently until the mixture begins to thicken, about 8 minutes.

6. Remove from the heat and stir in the Parmesan and roasted garlic.

7. ASSEMBLE AND BAKE THE PIZZA: Roll out the pizza dough into a 12-inch disc. Transfer the dough to a pizza pan, or if using a pizza stone, transfer the dough to the stone using a pizza peel.

8. Leaving an open edge around the outside, top the dough with the roasted garlic Alfredo sauce, Canadian bacon, pickles, mozzarella, and Parmesan.

9. Bake for 18 to 20 minutes, until the cheese is melted and the crust is golden. Let the pizza sit for about 3 minutes, then cut and serve.

10. Leftover pizza can be stored in an airtight container in the refrigerator for 1 to 2 days.

PIZZA

One 11- to 13-ounce (312 to 369 g) thin-crust pizza crust dough, store-bought or homemade

Flour, for rolling out the dough

25 to 30 slices (85 g) Canadian bacon

2 to 3 large dill pickles (1 cup / 145 g), thinly sliced

1 cup (113 g) shredded mozzarella cheese

¼ cup (25 g) grated Parmesan cheese

SOUPS AND SALADS

I DON'T KNOW what it is about me on social media, but folks always feel so empowered to tell me exactly how fattening my recipes are and how I am the reason diabetes exists. We're talking no-holds-barred, shame-your-momma-with-your-mouth, blame-me-specifically-for-Americans'-health-issues comments. After several years of this type of feedback I eventually resorted to creating Shirley, a character that handles calls at the Your Content Is Terrible Hotline. Because apparently, all my content is terrible. Shirley made it fun to deal with the naysayers, and to this day I get a kick out of negative comments.

Yes, there is a "salad" made of candy bars and marshmallows, and I will make no apologies for that. I just ask that you forgive me for the decadence. And if you can't, I have the number of a gal who can help you. ☺

I have no shame in my decadent baked goods or bacon-filled savory recipes, but I will begrudgingly admit that salads and soups are a welcome addition to any diet. Even mine. These salads are winning! And the soups—try the Dill Pickle Chowder first. Actually try the Lasagna Soup first! Never mind. I trust you will make the best choice for you.

POTATO SOUP

I kinda wanted to call this "Potato Soup Hot Dish," but I had a feeling I would confuse some folks. And why on earth would I feel compelled to do such a silly thing? I'll tell you, and then you have to promise to never tell anyone. I like making this soup and enjoying it in the traditional sense. Then, for leftovers, I will pop it into an oven-safe dish, load it with more cheese, and bake it for about 15 minutes, so it gets *really* thick and bubbly and golden on top. Try it!

PREP TIME: 20 minutes • **COOK TIME:** 40 minutes • **MAKES 8 SERVINGS**

1. In a large Dutch oven over medium heat, cook the bacon to the desired crispness. Remove the bacon to a plate lined with paper towels to drain. Do not drain the bacon grease from the Dutch oven. When the bacon is cool, crumble it. Set aside.

2. Add the onion to the Dutch oven and cook in the bacon grease until translucent, about 5 minutes, stirring often. Add the garlic and cook for 1 minute. Add the potatoes and bouillon cube. Toss to coat them in the grease. Cook, stirring occasionally, for 3 to 4 minutes. Add enough broth to just cover the potatoes. Cover, bring to a simmer, and cook until the potatoes are tender, about 20 minutes.

3. In a medium saucepan over medium heat, melt the butter. Whisk in the flour and cook, stirring constantly, for 1 to 2 minutes, until bubbling. Add the sour cream and 1 tablespoon of the chopped green onion and stir until heated through, about 2 minutes. Stir the sour cream mixture into the potato soup.

4. Remove about half the soup to a large bowl and use an immersion blender to puree it until smooth. (You can also use a blender—just be careful!) Return the soup to the Dutch oven.

5. Add the chili powder and half the bacon. Stir to combine, then add salt and pepper to taste.

6. Divide the soup among individual bowls and garnish with the remaining crumbled bacon, remaining green onion, and the cheese.

7. Leftovers can be stored in an airtight container in the refrigerator for 3 or 4 days.

3 or 4 thick-cut bacon slices (62 g), cut in half crosswise

1 small yellow or white onion, finely chopped (about ½ cup / 74 g)

3 garlic cloves, minced

8 russet potatoes, peeled and cut into ½-inch dice (about 8 cups / 1,120 g)

1 chicken bouillon cube, crushed

4 cups (960 ml) chicken broth, or enough to cover the potatoes

3 tablespoons unsalted butter

¼ cup (31 g) all-purpose flour

1 cup (230 g) sour cream

2 tablespoons finely chopped green onion

½ teaspoon chili powder

Kosher salt and freshly ground black pepper

Shredded cheddar cheese, for garnish

FRENCH ONION SOUP WITH HOMEMADE CROUTONS

I don't think I knowingly ate an onion until I was thirty years old. Onions were so *gross*. But then something happened, and all of a sudden I became obsessed with them. Caramelized, raw, fried, sautéed, chopped, grilled—you name it, I wanted it. Now that you know this about me, you know that my French Onion Soup must be perfect—or it's not worthy of these pages.

It. Is. Perfect. And with these delicious croutons, it's even more perfecter. *Perfecter* is totally a word, and you will agree when you make this.

See the photo on pages 78–79.

PREP TIME: 20 minutes • **COOK TIME:** 1 hour 15 minutes • **MAKES 4 SERVINGS**

4 tablespoons (½ stick / 57 g) salted butter

2 tablespoons olive oil

Kosher salt

2 large red onions, thinly sliced (about 5 cups / 740 g)

2 large sweet onions, thinly sliced (about 5 cups / 630 g)

4 cups (960 ml) chicken broth

4 cups (960 ml) beef broth

½ cup (120 ml) red wine

1 tablespoon Worcestershire sauce

2 fresh parsley sprigs

1 tablespoon balsamic vinegar

Freshly ground black pepper

4 cups (160 g) Homemade Croutons (recipe follows)

2 cups (226 g) shredded Gruyère cheese

2 cups (226 g) shredded Asiago cheese

1. In a large pot or Dutch oven over medium heat, melt the butter and oil. Add 1 teaspoon salt, the red onions, and sweet onions and stir to combine. Let the onions cook for about 10 minutes, until they stick a little to the bottom of the pan. Scrape them up and cook, uncovered and stirring occasionally, for about 35 minutes, until the onions are translucent, sticky, and almost syrupy.

2. Add the chicken broth, beef broth, red wine, and Worcestershire sauce to the pot. Bundle the parsley with kitchen twine and place it in the pot. Bring to a simmer and cook over medium heat for about 20 minutes, stirring occasionally. Remove and discard the parsley. Reduce the heat to low, mix in the balsamic vinegar, and season to taste with salt and pepper. Simmer for 5 minutes.

3. Preheat the oven broiler.

4. Arrange four large oven-safe bowls or crocks on a rimmed sheet pan and divide the soup among the bowls. Top each bowl with 5 or 6 croutons, ½ cup of the Gruyère cheese, and ½ cup of the Asiago cheese.

5. Broil until the cheese is bubbly and golden brown, 4 to 5 minutes. Keep a close eye on the tops!

6. Serve immediately.

7. Leftovers can be stored in an airtight container in the refrigerator for 3 or 4 days.

Homemade Croutons

PREP TIME: 5 minutes • **COOK TIME:** 10 to 15 minutes • **MAKES 4 TO 5 CUPS**

1. Preheat the oven to 350°F.

2. In a large oven-safe skillet over medium heat, melt the butter. Stir in the garlic and cook until fragrant, about 1 minute. Stir in the dried parsley. Add the bread cubes and toss to coat. (Depending on the size of the skillet, you may need to work in batches.)

3. Place the skillet into the oven and bake for 10 to 15 minutes, until the croutons are crispy and lightly browned. You are looking for a toasted-on-the-edges golden-brown appearance.

4. Use the croutons as directed in the soup recipe. You'll have plenty of extras for the soup or to use on a side salad.

5. Leftovers can be stored in an airtight container at room temperature for 3 or 4 days.

¾ cup (1½ sticks /170 g) salted butter

1 garlic clove, minced

1 tablespoon dried parsley

Nine 1-inch slices of French bread, cut into ½-inch cubes

FRENCH ONION SOUP WITH HOMEMADE CROUTONS, PAGE 76

ROASTED BROCCOLI AND CHEESE SOUP

The two best things about this recipe? Muenster and roasted broccoli. That's it. Those two. They absolutely dominate this simple soup and turn it into something beyond magical. The truth is that when I make this, I usually double the broccoli because I'll just snack on it. Roasted broccoli should not even be considered a vegetable, it's so delicious. But it's considered healthy, so go ahead and have a second bowl.

PREP TIME: 20 minutes • **COOK TIME:** 30 minutes • **MAKES 8 SERVINGS**

1. Preheat the oven to 400°F.

2. Place the broccoli on a large sheet pan and toss with the oil, salt, and pepper to coat evenly. Bake for 15 minutes, or until tender and lightly browned (5 minutes more for extra-crispy broccoli). Let cool slightly, finely chop (leaving a few big chunks if you prefer), and set aside.

3. In a large pot or Dutch oven over medium heat, melt the butter. Add the onion and cook, stirring often, for 3 to 5 minutes, until softened. Add the broth, bring to a simmer, and cook for 15 minutes. Reduce the heat to low.

4. Add the cheddar cheese and most of the muenster (reserve a small amount of muenster for garnish). Add the half-and-half and garlic powder and stir to combine.

5. In a small bowl, stir the cornstarch into 1 cup water until dissolved. Add the cornstarch slurry to the broth mixture and stir to combine.

6. Add the broccoli and cook over medium heat until the soup is thick and creamy, 5 to 10 minutes.

7. Divide the soup among bowls, garnish with the remaining muenster cheese, and serve.

8. Leftovers can be stored in an airtight container in the refrigerator for 3 or 4 days.

2 large heads of broccoli (about 1 pound / 454 g each)

2 to 4 tablespoons olive oil

1 teaspoon kosher salt

½ teaspoon freshly ground black pepper

½ cup (1 stick / 113 g) salted butter

1 large yellow onion, finely diced (about 1 cup / 148 g)

7 cups (1,680 ml) chicken broth

3 cups (339 g) shredded cheddar cheese

2 cups (226 g) shredded muenster cheese

2 cups (1 pint / 480 ml) half-and-half

1 tablespoon garlic powder

⅔ cup cornstarch

LASAGNA SOUP

As I mention more than once in this book . . . if you are Italian or prefer to stay true to authentic cuisine, look away! For all that is sacred and holy, avert your eyes, sweet child! If you are still here with me, *make this*. Folks have written to me for years about this recipe, praising it to high heaven. There's a reason. It's instant comfort food. And if you can, find the mafalda noodles—they're the icing on the cake! Or the noodle in the soup. You know what I mean.

PREP TIME: 10 minutes • **COOK TIME:** 20 minutes • **MAKES 12 SERVINGS**

1. In a large pot or Dutch oven over medium-high heat, heat the oil. Add the onion and sauté for 3 to 4 minutes, until partly translucent, stirring often. Add the garlic and sauté until fragrant, about 1 minute. Add the ground beef and sprinkle with the Italian seasoning, salt, and pepper. Cook until the meat is browned, stirring occasionally, 5 to 8 minutes. Drain the grease, if necessary. Return the pot to medium-high heat and add the pasta sauce, broth, and tomatoes and stir to combine. Add the pasta, bring to a simmer, and cook for 8 minutes, or until al dente. Add the heavy cream and cheeses and stir until combined.

2. Serve warm garnished with more of the cheeses and fresh parsley.

3. Leftovers can be stored in an airtight container in the refrigerator for 3 or 4 days.

NOTE: For a thinner soup, you can add up to 4 cups more beef broth.

1 tablespoon olive oil

1 large yellow onion, finely diced (about 1 cup / 148 g)

1 tablespoon minced garlic

2 pounds (908 g) lean ground beef

1 tablespoon Italian Seasoning (page 156)

2 teaspoons kosher salt

2 teaspoons freshly ground black pepper

One 24-ounce (680 g) jar store-bought pasta sauce

4 cups (960 ml) beef broth (see Note)

One 28-ounce (794 g) can crushed tomatoes, undrained

12 ounces (340 g) mafalda pasta or lasagna noodles, broken into small pieces

½ cup (120 ml) heavy cream

1 cup (113 g) shredded mozzarella cheese

1 cup (113 g) shredded Monterey Jack cheese blend, plus more for garnish (see Note)

Finely diced fresh parsley, for garnish

CHEESEBURGER SOUP WITH SESAME SEED CROUTONS

Meaty, cheesy, pickly, and pretty. I think my work here is done. But be forewarned: These homemade croutons are addictive. I've been known to snack on them and then have to make more when it's actually time to serve the soup. Whoops!

PREP TIME: 25 minutes • **COOK TIME:** 15 to 20 minutes • **MAKES 4 SERVINGS**

SOUP

1 to 2 tablespoons oil

1 pound (454 g) ground beef

1 large yellow onion, finely diced (about 1 cup / 148 g)

1 teaspoon garlic powder

½ teaspoon kosher salt

½ teaspoon ground black pepper

1 teaspoon Hamburger Seasoning Mix (page 157)

⅛ teaspoon ground mustard

1 tablespoon Worcestershire sauce

One 14.5-ounce (411 g) can diced tomatoes, undrained

1 cup (240 ml) chicken broth

¼ cup (37 g) finely diced dill pickles

CHEESE SAUCE

2 cups (480 ml) whole milk

½ cup (63 g) all-purpose flour

1 teaspoon kosher salt

3 ounces sharp cheddar cheese, shredded (about ⅔ cup)

½ teaspoon freshly ground black pepper

TOPPINGS

6 bacon slices, cooked until crisp, then crumbled (about 1 cup / 91 g)

1 to 2 small dill pickles, diced

Sesame Seed Croutons (recipe follows)

1. **MAKE THE SOUP:** In a large pot or Dutch oven over medium-high heat, heat the oil. Add the ground beef, onion, garlic powder, salt, pepper, hamburger seasoning, ground mustard, and Worcestershire sauce. Cook until almost all of the pink is gone from the beef, about 8 minutes, using a wooden spoon to break up the meat and combine the ingredients. Drain the grease, if necessary. Reduce the heat to low and return the pot to the stovetop. Add the tomatoes, broth, and pickles and bring to a simmer.

2. **MAKE THE CHEESE SAUCE:** Meanwhile, in a medium saucepan over medium heat, whisk ½ cup of the milk and the flour until thickened. Pour in the remaining milk, add the salt, and bring to a boil over medium heat, stirring frequently. Reduce the heat to low and simmer for 2 minutes, or until the mixture starts to thicken, stirring constantly. Remove from the heat.

3. Add the cheese and pepper and stir until the cheese melts.

4. **SERVE THE SOUP:** Whisk the cheese sauce into the simmering soup.

5. Divide among four bowls and garnish with bacon, pickles, and croutons.

6. Leftovers can be stored in an airtight container in the refrigerator for 3 or 4 days.

Sesame Seed Croutons

PREP TIME: 5 minutes • **COOK TIME:** 20 minutes • **MAKES 3 SERVINGS**

1. Preheat the oven to 350°F.

2. In a large oven-safe skillet over medium heat, melt the butter. Stir in the garlic and cook for 1 minute, or until fragrant. Stir in the dried parsley. Add the bread cubes and toss to coat. (Depending on the size of the skillet, you may need to work in batches.)

3. Place the skillet into the oven and bake for 10 to 15 minutes, until the croutons are crispy and lightly browned. You are looking for a toasted-on-the-edges golden-brown appearance.

4. Use the croutons as directed in the soup recipe. You'll have plenty of extras for the soup or to use on a side salad.

5. Leftovers can be stored in an airtight container at room temperature for 3 or 4 days.

½ cup (1 stick / 113 g) unsalted butter

1 teaspoon minced garlic

1 teaspoon dried parsley

3 sesame seed buns, cut into ½-inch cubes (about 3 cups / 180 g)

DILL PICKLE CHOWDER

Does that even sound good? I know it didn't to me when a family friend first made it. I prepared myself mentally and practiced my pleasantries, just assuming it would be terrible. But it was amazing. I had two bowls. In ten minutes. And would have had another had I not feared the judgment of everyone around. And please, if you're my child or my pastor, stop reading now. (It's a great hangover soup.)

PREP TIME: 20 minutes • **COOK TIME:** 50 minutes • **MAKES 4 SERVINGS**

1. In a large pot or Dutch oven over medium heat, cook the bacon until crispy, 15 to 20 minutes, depending on the size or cut of bacon. Remove the bacon to a plate lined with paper towels to drain. Let cool, then crumble. Leave about 2 tablespoons of bacon grease in the pan; discard the rest.

2. Add the onion to the pan and sauté over medium heat until softened, 8 to 10 minutes. Stir in the potatoes. Pour in the broth and bring to a boil. Reduce the heat to medium-low and simmer until the potatoes are tender, about 15 minutes. Remove half the mixture to a medium bowl and set it aside.

3. Using an immersion blender, process the remaining potato mixture until smooth.

4. In a small bowl, whisk the flour and milk to create a slurry. Stir the slurry into the blended soup.

5. Add the reserved potato mixture back into the pot. Stir in the ham, cheeses, pickles, and pickle juice. Bring to a simmer and cook until thickened, about 5 minutes. Season with the salt, black pepper, and cayenne.

6. Divide the soup among four bowls, top with the crumbled bacon, and serve.

7. Leftovers can be stored in an airtight container in the refrigerator for 3 or 4 days.

6 bacon slices (about 1 cup / 90 g)

1 small yellow onion, finely chopped (about ½ cup / 74 g)

5 large russet potatoes, peeled and cut into ½-inch cubes (about 5 cups / 700 g)

4 cups (960 ml) chicken broth

3 tablespoons all-purpose flour

1 cup (240 ml) whole milk

16 ounces thick-cut ham, diced (about 2 cups / 270 g)

1 cup (113 g) shredded cheddar cheese

1 cup (113 g) shredded Monterey Jack cheese

1 cup (143 g) finely chopped dill pickles

¾ cup (180 ml) pickle juice

1 teaspoon kosher salt

½ teaspoon ground black pepper

Pinch of cayenne pepper

JALAPEÑO CHICKEN SALAD

Whoa whoa whoa. Don't get scared by all the ingredients. I made the dressing from scratch, so it looks especially daunting. (You could definitely use store-bought.) The truth is, these crispy fried jalapeños could be a recipe all on their own—they're like an extra-spicy shoestring fry, and fantastic! They're also sometimes called Texas toothpicks. I just happen to love them the best when paired with a crisp, cool salad. So these three elements—salad, dressing, and fried jalapeños—are all amazing on their own, yet equally amazing together!

See the photo on page 90.

PREP TIME: 30 minutes • **CHILL TIME:** 2 hours • **COOK TIME:** 10 minutes • **MAKES 4 SERVINGS**

CRISPY FRIED JALAPEÑOS

1 cup (125 g) all-purpose flour, plus more as needed

Kosher salt

1 teaspoon freshly ground black pepper

1 teaspoon chili powder

1 teaspoon garlic powder

2 large eggs

1 cup (240 ml) light beer of your choice, plus more as needed

2 cups (480 ml) vegetable oil

5 or 6 large jalapeño peppers, seeded and cut lengthwise into skinny spears

SALAD

1 rotisserie chicken, skin removed, meat shredded (about 3 cups / 420 g)

1 teaspoon chipotle powder

½ teaspoon freshly squeezed lime juice

⅛ teaspoon ground cumin

⅛ teaspoon cayenne pepper

½ teaspoon garlic powder

2 heads of romaine lettuce, roughly chopped (about 8 cups / 600 g)

1 Roma tomato, finely diced (about ⅔ cup / 120 g)

1 small red onion, finely diced (about ½ cup / 74 g)

3 bacon slices, cooked until crisp, then crumbled (about ½ cup / 45 g)

1 large ripe Haas avocado, halved, pitted, peeled, and cut into thin slices

One 15.25-ounce (432 g) can corn kernels, drained

1 tablespoon finely chopped fresh cilantro

½ cup Jalapeño Ranch Dressing (recipe follows), plus more as needed

1. **MAKE THE CRISPY FRIED JALAPEÑOS:** In a large bowl, whisk the flour, 1 teaspoon salt, the black pepper, chili powder, garlic powder, eggs, and beer. (The batter should be slightly thinner than pancake batter; adjust with a bit more flour or beer as needed.)

2. In a deep fryer or large skillet, heat the oil to 365°F. (Try to maintain that temperature all throughout frying.)

3. Dip the jalapeños in the batter and completely coat all sides.

4. Place a few well-coated jalapeño spears at a time in the deep fryer and fry for about 2 minutes. The jalapeños are fully cooked when they are golden brown and crispy and float to the top of the oil. (They will continue to brown a bit when removed from the oil.) Remove the jalapeño spears using a spider or slotted spoon and set them on a plate lined with paper towels to drain. When cool enough to handle, taste and add more salt if desired.

5. **ASSEMBLE THE SALAD:** In a medium bowl, combine the shredded chicken, chipotle powder, lime juice, cumin, cayenne, and garlic powder.

6. In a large bowl, combine the romaine lettuce, tomato, onion, bacon, avocado, corn, cilantro, and dressing. Add the seasoned chicken and toss to coat. Add more dressing to taste.

7. Top with the crispy fried jalapeños. Serve immediately.

Jalapeño Ranch Dressing

MAKES 4 CUPS

½ teaspoon onion powder

¼ teaspoon kosher salt

¼ teaspoon freshly ground black pepper

1 tablespoon minced fresh cilantro

2 cups (460 g) mayonnaise

1 cup (460 g) sour cream

1 teaspoon dried chives

1 teaspoon dried parsley

1 teaspoon dried dill

1 teaspoon garlic powder

1 or 2 medium jalapeño peppers, roughly chopped (about ⅔ cup / 98 g)

1 medium tomato, roughly chopped (about 1 cup / 180 g)

1 large ripe Haas avocado, halved, peeled, pitted, and roughly chopped

Combine all the ingredients in a blender and blend on high speed until smooth. Transfer to an airtight container and refrigerate for at least 2 hours before serving. Store the dressing in an airtight container in the refrigerator for up to 5 days.

JALAPEÑO CHICKEN SALAD, PAGE 88

MIDWESTERN WEDGE SALAD, PAGE 92

MIDWESTERN WEDGE SALAD

There has never been a wedge salad like this! The secret is the pork belly. I perfected it in the oven, but you can also use a grill, smoker, or air fryer. (Honestly the air fryer is fastest and easiest!) The combination of the pork belly and crisp lettuce is something I think about before I go to sleep. Simply magical.

See the photo on page 91.

PREP TIME: 30 minutes • **COOK TIME:** 2 hours 20 minutes • **MAKES 4 SERVINGS**

PORK BELLY

1½ pounds (681 g) pork belly

Kosher salt

2 teaspoons freshly ground black pepper

2 tablespoons light brown sugar

2 teaspoons garlic powder

SALAD

Head of iceberg lettuce

¼ cup (28 g) blue cheese crumbles

8 ounces cherry tomatoes, halved (about 1 cup / 227 g)

1 small red onion, finely diced (about ½ cup / 74 g)

Homemade Croutons (page 77)

1 cup (250 g) blue cheese or ranch dressing

⅛ teaspoon freshly ground black pepper

Finely diced fresh chives, for garnish

1. Preheat the oven to 300°F. Line a sheet pan with parchment paper and top with a wire rack.

2. **BAKE THE PORK BELLY:** Use paper towels to dry off the pork belly. Use a toothpick to poke a lot of holes into the fatty side (the more holes you poke, the crispier the pork belly will be after cooking).

3. In a small bowl, mix together 2 teaspoons salt, the pepper, brown sugar, and garlic powder. Flip the pork belly over and season with half the brown sugar mixture. Massage the mixture into the meat.

4. Set the pork belly fatty side up on the prepared baking rack. Make a foil wrap for the pork that's about 3 × 20 inches. Tightly wrap the foil around the sides of the pork belly to make a little foil "fence" that extends above the fatty side of the pork belly by 1 to 2 inches.

5. Pour ½ cup salt over the pork within the confines of the "fence," making sure the entire surface is covered. The foil will keep it in place while baking.

6. Bake for 2 hours. Most of the salt will have formed a solidified crust.

7. Remove the pork from the oven and increase the oven temperature to 475°F.

8. Remove the foil and the salt crust from the pork belly, carefully brushing away as much excess salt as you can. Remove the wire rack from the sheet pan. Cut the meat into 1- to 2-inch bites and place them in a single layer on the parchment-lined sheet pan. Sprinkle the meat with the remaining brown sugar mixture.

9. Bake for 20 minutes, or until the fatty side of the meat starts to crisp and bubble. Remove from the oven and tent with clean foil to keep warm.

10. **ASSEMBLE THE SALAD:** While the pork is in the oven, prepare the rest of the salad. Remove the core and any outer wilted leaves from the lettuce. Chop the lettuce in half and then in half again, making 4 wedges.

11. Plate the wedges and top them with the blue cheese crumbles, warm pork belly, tomato, and onion. Top each salad with croutons, the dressing of your choice, and pepper. Garnish with chives.

12. Serve and enjoy.

13. Leftover pork belly can be stored in an airtight container in the refrigerator for 3 or 4 days.

CHEESEBURGER SALAD

What the heck is a cheeseburger salad anyway? The recipe seems weird in concept, but once you try it, it will make perfect sense. It tastes exactly like a cheeseburger from a super-popular fast-food restaurant. I was delighted at the first bite and felt it was my civic duty to go back for more. If you happen to be a low-carb eater, this is the salad for you. Perfectly seasoned ground beef and all the typical burger fixins make this salad a keeper.

PREP TIME: 20 minutes • **COOK TIME:** 8 to 10 minutes • **MAKES 4 SERVINGS**

1. In a medium skillet over medium heat, add the ground beef, garlic powder, hamburger seasoning, salt, and pepper. Cook, stirring occasionally, until no pink remains in the ground beef, 8 to 10 minutes. Remove from the heat and drain, if necessary. Set aside and cover to keep warm.

2. **MAKE THE DRESSING:** In a medium bowl, whisk the yogurt, vinegar, mustard, ketchup, and paprika. If you think the dressing has too strong of a mustard taste, add the sugar.

3. **ASSEMBLE THE SALAD:** In a large bowl, make a bed of the lettuce. Add the cheese, tomatoes, pickles, onion, and beef. Pour the dressing over the salad. Toss and serve.

1 pound (454 g) ground beef

1 teaspoon garlic powder

½ teaspoon Hamburger Seasoning Mix (page 157)

Pinch of kosher salt

Pinch of freshly ground black pepper

DRESSING

½ cup (143 g) plain whole milk Greek yogurt

1 tablespoon red wine vinegar

2 teaspoons yellow mustard

1 teaspoon ketchup

½ teaspoon smoked paprika

1 teaspoon granulated sugar (optional)

SALAD

2 heads of romaine lettuce, chopped (about 8 cups / 600 g)

1 cup (113 g) shredded cheddar cheese

5 ounces grape tomatoes, halved (about 1 cup / 155 g)

¼ cup (37 g) sliced baby dill pickles

¼ medium red onion, thinly sliced (about ¼ cup / 37 g)

CANDY BAR APPLE SALAD

If you've never heard of this, you are judging me so hard right now. A candy salad? Yes. But the truth is, I have about a hundred variations of this salad on my website, and they are all amazing. I mean, only if you appreciate how the Midwest will take any food and mix it together and call it a salad.

PREP TIME: 20 minutes • **MAKES 12 SERVINGS**

1. Fill a large bowl about halfway with water. Add the salt. Place the apples in the salted water while you prepare the pudding mixture. (This keeps the apples from browning.)

2. In another large bowl, whisk the milk and pudding mix for 2 minutes, or until thickened. Let sit for about 2 minutes, until softly set. Gently fold in the whipped topping until smooth.

3. Drain the apples. Fold the apples, candy bar pieces, and marshmallows into the pudding mixture. Transfer to a large serving dish and refrigerate until serving.

4. Leftovers can be stored in an airtight container in the refrigerator for 3 or 4 days.

1 teaspoon kosher salt

6 large Granny Smith apples, cored and cubed (about 8 cups / 1,400 g)

1½ cups (360 ml) whole milk

One 3.4-ounce (96 g) package instant vanilla pudding mix

One 8-ounce (227 g) carton frozen whipped topping, thawed

One 10.59-ounce (300 g) bag Snickers fun-size candy bars, roughly chopped

2 cups (100 g) mini marshmallows

BLUEBERRY SPINACH SALAD

This salad was conceived on one of those "use what you have in the fridge" days. I had never had a blueberry in a salad before, and certainly never with spinach. Boy, was I missing out! I highly recommend making it as is and then modifying individual ingredients to fit your tastes.

PREP TIME: 20 minutes • **MARINATE:** 1 to 3 hours • **COOK TIME:** 15 minutes • **MAKES 4 SERVINGS**

1. In a large bowl or gallon-size resealable plastic bag, combine the vinegar, 1 tablespoon of the oil, the garlic, salt, pepper, and honey. Add the chicken and marinate in the refrigerator for 1 to 3 hours.

2. When ready to cook, heat the remaining 1 tablespoon oil in a large skillet over medium heat. When the oil is hot, cook the chicken for 6 to 8 minutes per side, until the internal temperature of the chicken reaches 165°F. Remove from the heat and let the chicken cool for about 5 minutes, then cut into bite-size chunks.

3. In a large bowl, combine the spinach, blueberries, cherry tomatoes, cranberries, sunflower seeds, and shallot. Place the cut chicken on top. (I like to arrange the ingredients in sections to look pretty and then toss the salad at the table when ready to serve.) Pour the dressing over the salad. (Start with less dressing than you think you'll need; you can always add more.)

4. Toss the salad and serve immediately.

1 cup balsamic vinegar

2 tablespoons olive oil

1 teaspoon minced garlic

½ teaspoon kosher salt

¼ teaspoon freshly ground black pepper

¼ cup honey

Two 4-ounce (227 g total) boneless skinless chicken breasts

8 ounces (30 g) baby spinach

1 cup (190 g) fresh blueberries

8 ounces cherry tomatoes, halved (about 1 cup / 227 g)

¼ cup (33 g) dried cranberries

¼ cup (28 g) sunflower seeds

1 medium shallot, finely diced (about ⅓ cup / 49 g)

½ cup Homemade Poppyseed Dressing (page 173), or to taste

HOT DISH

WHAT THE HECK is hot dish?

That is what my SEO (social engine optimization) guy asks when he shakes his head at my use of *hot dish* instead of *casserole*. "No one is searching for hot dish on the internet," he tells me. "Only casserole! Change it to casserole. People understand what a casserole is!" Apparently if I want Google to recognize my recipes I have to use the more commonly known term, which has been nothing short of an ongoing mental betrayal to my Minnesotan roots.

Hot dish is commonly known in Minnesota and North Dakota and not many other places. It's actually the Official State Food of Minnesota! Unofficially, of course. Folks from Wisconsin scoff at the word (they scoff at everything we do, to be honest) and South Dakotans, not to be confused as southern North Dakotans, claim *casserole* as their preferred word.

When we refer to hot dish, it is *usually* involving Tater Tots. It shouldn't be from scratch, it should incorporate a can of cream-of-something, and it shouldn't be pretty. Half the time it doesn't even need to taste good, as our taste buds are fueled by nostalgia alone.

I broke from the mold with my Potato Tot Hot Dish, as I made my own cheese sauce. I also deviated away from making "Tater Tot–only" hot dish; in my mind, hot dish is any dish that is served hot for dinner. These hot dish recipes are a love letter to my roots combined with a desire to make food that tastes amazing.

MEAT RAFFLE HOT DISH

I visited New York for an event I did with Facebook, and while talking to a very high-up Facebook professional, I mentioned meat raffles. The look of bewilderment was the first clue I had that meat raffles were not a common thing. That VIP made a quick exit from our odd conversation, and I made it my mission to tell the world about meat raffles. It is simply this: You go to a bar and buy a ticket for a dollar, and then a sweet gal will spin the wheel and announce who won that round. If it was you, you get to sit at the bar with a pound of ground beef or whatever cut of beef they're giving away that night. Folks around here love meat raffles, and raffles in general, and this recipe is the perfect way to enjoy it. Quick, easy, and delish.

PREP TIME: 15 minutes • **COOK TIME:** 40 minutes • **MAKES 8 SERVINGS**

1. Preheat the oven to 350°F.

2. In a large, oven-safe skillet over medium heat, add the ground beef, onion, salt, and pepper and cook over medium heat for about 5 minutes. It's okay if the beef is still a little pink. Remove the skillet from the heat and drain, if necessary. Return the skillet to the stovetop, add the garlic, and cook until fragrant, about 1 minute. Add the milk, cream of mushroom soup, and corn and mix well. Set aside.

3. Grease a 9 × 13-inch baking dish with nonstick spray. Pour the uncooked macaroni into the baking dish and spoon the hamburger mixture on top, ensuring that all the pasta is completely covered (especially at the sides). Top evenly with the cheese.

4. Cover the pan with foil and bake for 20 minutes. Remove the foil and bake for 15 minutes more, or until the cheese is melted.

5. Serve hot.

6. Leftovers can be stored in an airtight container in the refrigerator for 3 or 4 days.

1 pound (454 g) ground beef

1 small yellow onion, finely diced (about ½ cup / 74 g)

1 teaspoon kosher salt

½ teaspoon freshly ground black pepper

1 teaspoon minced garlic

1½ cups (360 ml) whole milk

One 10.5-ounce (298 g) can cream of mushroom soup

1 cup (165 g) canned corn kernels, drained

Nonstick spray

2 cups (210 g) elbow macaroni

2 cups (226 g) shredded sharp cheddar cheese

SUMMER CORN HOT DISH

Corn. The world's perfect vegetable. Or is it a starch? Whatever it is technically, I love it. There's no bad way to make it. Usually I drown it in butter and bacon, but this is a "fresher" variation. The addition of the basil adds a lightness to the flavor that I can't help but love.

PREP TIME: 15 minutes • **COOK TIME:** 50 minutes • **MAKES 9 SERVINGS**

1. Preheat the oven to 350°F. Grease an 8 × 8-inch baking dish with nonstick spray.

2. In a large bowl, combine the corn, egg, half-and-half, salt, ½ cup of the Parmesan, 1 teaspoon of the basil, the jalapeño, and shallot. Stir to combine.

3. Transfer the corn mixture to the prepared baking dish. Use a small offset spatula to spread it into an even layer. Top evenly with the remaining ½ cup Parmesan.

4. Bake for 40 minutes. Top evenly with the mozzarella and bake for 10 more minutes, or until the cheese is melted.

5. Garnish with the remaining 1 teaspoon basil and serve.

6. Leftovers can be stored in an airtight container in the refrigerator for 3 or 4 days.

Nonstick spray

Three 15.25-ounce (1.3 kg total) cans corn kernels, drained

1 large egg

¼ cup (60 ml) half-and-half

1 teaspoon kosher salt

1 cup (100 g) finely grated Parmesan cheese

2 teaspoons finely chopped fresh basil leaves

1 medium jalapeño pepper, seeded and finely diced (about ¼ cup / 23 g; leave the seeds in for more heat)

1 medium shallot, finely diced (about ⅓ cup / 49 g)

1 cup (113 g) shredded mozzarella cheese

MONA'S GOULASH

My friend Autumn shared her mom's goulash recipe with me, and I knew I had to share it with the world. Here is what Autumn wrote when I asked for more details about this famous recipe: "My mom, Mona, is a woman like no other, and her goulash recipe follows suit. Growing up on a small midwestern farm, we were never without company. Constantly being surrounded by family and friends meant that the extra leaves in the table were always in place. That table seated eight, and yet at nearly every meal, we managed to squeeze in twelve. With hungry mouths to feed, my mom would always whip up a warm and cozy dish that could feed a small army. Her goulash was by far the most requested menu item, and to this day it's one of my absolute favorite things to eat."

PREP TIME: 15 minutes   •   **COOK TIME:** 20 minutes   •   **MAKES 8 SERVINGS**

1. Cook the pasta according to the package directions. Drain and set aside.

2. In a 15-inch skillet or a large pot over medium heat, heat the oil. Add the bell pepper and onion and sauté until soft, 5 to 8 minutes. Add the ground beef, salt, and pepper and cook, breaking up the meat with a wooden spoon, until no longer pink, about 8 minutes. Remove the skillet from the heat and drain. Return the skillet to the stovetop and add the garlic, cooking until fragrant, about 1 minute. Add the tomato soup, diced tomatoes, and cooked noodles.

3. Stir everything together and simmer on low for 5 minutes, or until everything is cooked through.

4. Serve hot.

5. Leftovers can be stored in an airtight container in the refrigerator for 3 or 4 days.

1 pound (454 g) elbow macaroni

1 tablespoon olive oil

1 green bell pepper, finely diced (about 1 cup / 150 g)

1 small yellow onion, finely chopped (about ½ cup / 74 g)

1½ pounds (681 g) ground beef

2 teaspoons kosher salt

1 teaspoon freshly ground black pepper

1 teaspoon minced garlic

Two 10.75-ounce (610 g total) cans tomato soup

One 28-ounce (794 g) can diced tomatoes, undrained

MINNESOTA MEAT AND MASHED POTATOES HOT DISH, PAGE 110

MINNESOTA MEAT AND MASHED POTATOES HOT DISH

Shepherd's pie. This is basically what people think of as shepherd's pie, even though it's made with beef. So why didn't I call it that? Simply put, *we* didn't call it that. When I was growing up, everything was hot dish. Even if it was a cold dish, it was hot dish. And this classic, but slightly modified version, was hot dish. I don't make the rules here, folks.

One thing I daresay is worth trying is the skins-on mashed potatoes. That combination seems unique to the Midwest, and as few things are, I have to hold on to them tightly. Plus, it's stinkin' delicious.

See the photo on pages 108–109.

PREP TIME: 15 minutes • **COOK TIME:** 35 minutes • **MAKES 8 SERVINGS**

Nonstick spray

1 teaspoon olive oil

1 small yellow onion, finely chopped (about ½ cup / 74 g)

2 garlic cloves, minced

2 pounds (908 g) ground beef

One 15.25-ounce (432 g) can corn kernels, drained

⅓ cup (75 g) ketchup

1 teaspoon kosher salt

½ teaspoon freshly ground black pepper

Skins-On Mashed Potatoes (recipe follows)

1. Preheat the oven to 350°F. Grease a 9 × 13-inch baking dish with nonstick spray.

2. In a large skillet over medium heat, heat the oil. Add the onion and garlic and sauté until translucent, 5 to 6 minutes. Be sure to not burn the garlic. Add the ground beef and cook, breaking up the meat with a wooden spoon, until no longer pink, about 8 minutes. Remove the skillet from the heat and drain, if necessary. Return the skillet to the stovetop and add the corn, ketchup, salt, and pepper. Stir well.

3. Transfer the meat to the prepared baking dish and press down to spread it into an even layer. Carefully spread the mashed potatoes over the meat and smooth them out.

4. Bake, uncovered, until the top is lightly golden, about 30 minutes.

5. Serve hot.

6. Leftovers can be stored in an airtight container in the refrigerator for 3 or 4 days.

Skins-On Mashed Potatoes

PREP TIME: 15 minutes • **COOK TIME:** 25 minutes • **MAKES 5½ CUPS**

1. Put the potatoes in a large pot and cover with salted water. Cover the pot and bring to a boil over medium-high heat. Boil, uncovered, until fork-tender, about 25 minutes. Drain the potatoes and return them to the pot off the heat.

2. Lightly mash the potatoes. Add the butter, cream, and salt and pepper to taste and mash to your desired consistency of creaminess.

3. Leftovers can be stored in an airtight container in the refrigerator for 3 or 4 days.

6 pounds (2.7 kg) unpeeled red potatoes, washed and cut into 2-inch chunks

Kosher salt

1 cup (2 sticks /227 g) unsalted butter, at room temperature

1 cup (240 ml) heavy cream

Freshly ground black pepper

CHICKEN POT PIE

This is the recipe that my husband uses when he makes two dozen full-size pot pies at a time. You read that right. And it gets even better . . . often he'll be on an ice fishing trip with his childhood friends and they'll make sixty-plus pies at once. A group of grown men, ice fishing and drinking, making the best chicken pot pie ever. They vacuum-seal the pies and then each take a dozen home. I never knew men to do such things on a "boys' weekend," but you know I'm thankful that I married one who does. I'll never complain about a boys' weekend ever again!

PREP TIME: 1 hour • **COOK TIME:** 1 hour 25 minutes • **MAKES 8 SERVINGS**

1. Preheat the oven to 375°F.

2. In a medium saucepan over medium heat, heat the chicken broth. Add the carrots and potatoes and cook for 10 to 15 minutes, until fork tender. Add the onion, peas, celery, and corn and cook for 3 minutes, or until softened. Cover and set aside to keep warm.

3. In a large saucepan over medium heat, melt the butter. Add the flour and whisk to combine. Cook, whisking constantly, for about 1 minute, until golden brown. Add the apple cider, milk, salt, and spices, bring to a simmer, and cook until thickened, about 5 minutes. Add the cooked vegetables and chicken, mix well, and simmer over low heat for 20 minutes.

4. Meanwhile, on a lightly floured surface, roll out the pie crust into two 11-inch discs. Lay 1 disc in a 9-inch pie pan and settle it into the edge of the pan. Pour the chicken mixture into the pan over the crust. Lay the second disc on top. Use a knife to trim the dough around the edge of the pie pan, then use a fork to crimp the edges of the 2 pie crusts together. Brush the top of the crust lightly with the egg wash. Make 4 to 5 small cuts in the top crust to vent.

5. Set the pie on a sheet pan (to catch any drips) and bake for 30 to 40 minutes, until the top crust is golden brown (store-bought crusts may need less time).

6. Leftovers can be stored in an airtight container in the refrigerator for 3 or 4 days.

1 cup (240 ml) chicken broth

2 medium carrots, finely chopped (about 1 cup / 130 g)

1 medium red potato, finely chopped (about 1 cup / 150 g)

1 large yellow onion, finely chopped (about 1 cup / 148 g)

1 cup (134 g) frozen peas

2 celery stalks, finely chopped (about 1 cup / 100 g)

One 15.25-ounce (432 g) can corn kernels, drained

¼ cup (½ stick / 57 g) unsalted butter

¼ cup (31 g) all-purpose flour, plus more as needed to roll out the dough

¼ cup (60 ml) apple cider

1 cup (240 ml) whole milk

2 teaspoons kosher salt

1 teaspoon dried parsley

1 teaspoon paprika

1 teaspoon dried oregano

1 teaspoon freshly ground black pepper

3 cups (420 g) bite-size cooked chicken chunks

1 recipe Never-Fail Pie Crust (page 239) or store-bought pie crust

1 large egg, whisked, for an egg wash

POTATO TOT HOT DISH

Some of you may know this as Tater Tot *casserole*, but you're wrong. Okay, okay, that was a bit harsh. I can get possessive of my hot dish, all right? This recipe is based on how I had it growing up, with the exception of the cheese sauce. You might think it odd, but if you do think it odd to add cheese sauce to anything and everything, maybe we need to rethink the friendship. More cheese sauce, please!

PREP TIME: 30 minutes • **COOK TIME:** 1 hour 5 minutes • **MAKES 8 SERVINGS**

1. Preheat the oven to 350°F. Line a sheet pan with parchment paper. Grease a 9 × 13-inch baking dish with nonstick spray.

2. Place the Tater Tots in a single layer on the prepared sheet pan. Bake for 15 minutes (this is just to pre-crisp them). Set aside to cool.

3. Meanwhile, in a large skillet over medium heat, cook the ground beef with the onion, garlic powder, salt, and pepper, breaking up the meat with a wooden spoon, until no longer pink, about 8 minutes. Remove the skillet from the heat and drain. Return the skillet to the stovetop and stir in the cream of mushroom soup and frozen mixed vegetables.

4. Pour the beef mixture into the prepared baking dish and smooth it out into an even layer. Pour the cheese sauce over the beef mixture. Top with an even layer of Tater Tots.

5. Bake for 40 to 50 minutes, until bubbling and the Tater Tots are browned. Serve hot.

6. Leftovers can be stored in an airtight container in the refrigerator for 3 or 4 days.

Nonstick spray

One 32-ounce (908 g) package frozen Tater Tots

1 pound (454 g) lean ground beef

1 small yellow onion, finely diced (½ cup / 74 g)

½ teaspoon garlic powder

½ teaspoon kosher salt

½ teaspoon freshly ground black pepper

One 10.5-ounce (298 g) can cream of mushroom soup

One 16-ounce (907 g) bag frozen mixed vegetables

1 cup Homemade Cheese Sauce (recipe follows)

HOMEMADE CHEESE SAUCE

This cheese sauce is a great addition to any hot dish. It's also terrific as a dip for French fries or mixed with cooked pasta for a quick mac and cheese.

In a medium saucepan over medium heat, whisk ½ cup (120 ml) whole milk and 8 teaspoons (21 g) all-purpose flour. Pour in 1½ cups (360 ml) whole milk and 1 teaspoon kosher salt and bring to a boil over medium heat, stirring frequently. Reduce the heat to low and simmer for 2 minutes, stirring constantly.

The mixture will start to thicken. Remove from the heat and stir in 1⅓ cups (151 g) shredded sharp cheddar cheese and ½ teaspoon black pepper until the cheese melts. Refrigerate leftover sauce for up to 4 days and reheat when ready to use.

CHEESY ENCHILADA NOODLE SKILLET

Oh my heck, I love this dish. Please make it and then tell me you love it too. This just might be the spiciest thing in this book! Is it okay to admit that? I am just not an overly spicy kinda girl. But this dish . . . it's *flavorful.*

Quick tip for ya—you can ignore the measurements and just add the whole can of corn. My taste testers say 1 cup is perfect, but I can't stand having leftover canned goods in my fridge, so just add the whole thing.

PREP TIME: 20 minutes • **COOK TIME:** 15 minutes • **MAKES 8 SERVINGS**

1. Cook the pasta according to the package instructions. Drain and set aside.

2. In a large skillet over medium heat, heat the oil. Add the ground beef, onion, and jalapeños and cook until almost all the pink is gone, breaking up the meat with a wooden spoon, about 8 minutes. Remove the skillet from the heat and drain. Return the skillet to the stovetop and add the garlic, cooking until fragrant, about 1 minute. Add the cooked pasta, corn, black beans, enchilada sauce, chili powder, cumin, salt, pepper, and 1 cup of the cheese. Stir for 2 to 3 minutes, until heated through. Top with the remaining 1 cup cheese, cover the pan, and cook until the cheese has melted, 2 to 3 minutes.

3. Serve hot, garnished with cilantro.

4. Leftovers can be stored in an airtight container in the refrigerator for 3 or 4 days.

8 ounces (227 g) elbow macaroni

2 tablespoons olive oil

1 pound (454 g) ground beef

1 small yellow onion, finely diced (about ½ cup / 74 g)

2 medium jalapeño peppers, seeded and finely diced (⅓ cup / 30 g)

1½ teaspoons minced garlic

1 cup (165 g) canned corn kernels, drained

1 cup (172 g) canned black beans, rinsed and drained

One 19-ounce (539 g) can mild (or spicy) enchilada sauce

½ teaspoon chili powder

½ teaspoon ground cumin

1 teaspoon kosher salt

¼ teaspoon freshly ground black pepper

2 cups (226 g) grated Mexican-blend cheese

2 tablespoons chopped fresh cilantro, for garnish

MAIN DISHES

WHEN I WENT to culinary school I couldn't wait to dive headfirst in the main course. Just kidding! I never went to culinary school. I went to the "What Am I Going to Feed My Hungry Family?" school of hard knocks. I started from scratch, quite literally. Not knowing what to make or how to make it! After mastering a few staple dishes over and over and over again, I was able to improve upon some of our typical recipes.

Baked pork chops were upgraded to French Onion Pork Chops, and macaroni and cheese was elevated to Pulled Pork Mac and Cheese, which will blow your mind.

I couldn't help myself and added a few nontraditional options, like Deconstructed French Onion Burger and Surprise Meatloaf, which surprises me every single time. It's the best (and only) surprise I want to be associated with meatloaf! It's a good surprise, promise.

GROUND BEEF

SPAGHETTI PIZZA   121

SALISBURY STEAK   125

HAMBURGER STROGANOFF   127

SURPRISE MEATLOAF   128

CREAMY DILL PICKLE
BURGER   131

DECONSTRUCTED FRENCH
ONION BURGER   132

CRANBERRY WILD RICE
MEATBALLS   135

CHICKEN

BUFFALO STUFFED
CHICKEN   137

STUFFED FRENCH ONION
CHICKEN   138

CHICKEN ALFREDO WITH
BRUSSELS SPROUTS   141

SUN-DRIED TOMATO CHICKEN
BITES   143

PORK

FRENCH ONION PORK
CHOPS   145

CHERRY PORK CHOPS   147

JALAPEÑO POPPER–STUFFED
PORK   149

OVEN PULLED PORK   151

PULLED PORK MAC AND
CHEESE   153

SEASONINGS

HOMEMADE TACO
SEASONING   156

ITALIAN SEASONING   156

HAMBURGER SEASONING
MIX   157

HOMEMADE RANCH
SEASONING MIX   157

SPAGHETTI PIZZA

If you love authenticity in recipes, look away now! But if you grew up in a very small midwestern town like I did, chances are you didn't eat authentic Italian dishes on a regular basis. That is where this recipe was born.

Here goes: I only ever eat spaghetti *on* garlic toast. You read that right. I pile the spaghetti on my garlic toast. I refuse to eat spaghetti in public to avoid the stares and disdain. After momming for a few years, I happened to observe my children eating spaghetti and noticed that they were eating it just like me. And I died a little inside, knowing that it would be a tough conversation with others should they ever eat spaghetti in public. So I decided to make it as classy as my wee brain could muster—and Spaghetti Pizza was born. You're supposed to eat it on bread, and it just happens to taste amazing. Stop judging me. Okay, you can judge me as long as you try this first.

PREP TIME: 20 minutes • **RESTING TIME:** 1 hour 5 minutes • **COOK TIME:** 1 hour • **MAKES 8 SERVINGS**

1. **MAKE THE FOCACCIA BREAD CRUST:** In a large bowl, combine the yeast, warm water, and sugar. Stir and let rest for 5 minutes.

2. In a small bowl, combine the ⅓ cup oil, the Italian seasoning, garlic, and ½ teaspoon of the salt. Pour half the oil mixture into the yeast mixture. Set the remaining oil mixture aside. Add the flour and stir to combine. The dough will be sticky.

3. Grease a large bowl with olive oil. Place the dough in the bowl and cover with a tea towel. Rest for 1 hour, or until the dough has doubled in size.

4. **MAKE THE SPAGHETTI TOPPING:** In a large saucepan or Dutch oven over medium heat, add the ground beef, salt, pepper, onion, and bell pepper. Cook, stirring often, until the meat is browned and the vegetables are tender, 8 to 10 minutes. Drain, if necessary. Return the saucepan to the stovetop and add the garlic, cooking until fragrant, about 1 minute. Add the diced tomatoes, tomato sauce, tomato paste, oregano, basil, and sugar and stir to combine. Bring to a simmer and cook for at least 20 minutes and up to 1 hour, stirring occasionally.

5. **BAKE THE FOCACCIA:** Preheat the oven to 450°F.

FOCACCIA BREAD CRUST

1 teaspoon active dry yeast

1 cup (240 ml) warm water (105°F to 115°F)

2 tablespoons granulated sugar

⅓ cup (73 g) plus 1 teaspoon olive oil and more for greasing

1 tablespoon Italian Seasoning (page 156)

2 teaspoons minced garlic

1 teaspoon sea salt

2½ cups (313 g) all-purpose flour

SPAGHETTI TOPPING

1 pound (454 g) ground beef

1 teaspoon kosher salt

½ teaspoon freshly ground black pepper

(continued)

1 small yellow onion, finely chopped (about ½ cup / 74 g)

1 green bell pepper, finely diced (about ½ cup / 75 g)

1 tablespoon minced garlic

One 28-ounce (794 g) can diced tomatoes

One 16-ounce (454 g) can tomato sauce

One 6-ounce (170 g) can tomato paste

2 teaspoons dried oregano

2 teaspoons dried basil

1 teaspoon granulated sugar

1 pound (454 g) spaghetti

6. Pour the reserved oil mixture into a 12-inch oven-safe skillet. Use a pastry brush to coat the bottom and sides of the skillet with the oil.

7. Place the dough in the skillet and use your clean fingers to gently work the dough out to the edges, then to create dimples in the dough. Brush the dough with the remaining 1 teaspoon oil, then sprinkle with the remaining ½ teaspoon sea salt.

8. Bake for 18 to 20 minutes, until the top is golden brown.

9. **ASSEMBLE THE PIZZA:** While the focaccia is baking, cook the pasta according to the package instructions. Drain and set aside.

10. Remove the focaccia from the oven and top with the cooked noodles and then the spaghetti sauce.

11. Slice into wedges and serve warm.

12. Leftover pizza can be stored in an airtight container in the refrigerator for 1 to 2 days.

SALISBURY STEAK

I grew up without much—my very first memory is falling off the top bunk bed in our trailer. But my mom was a master at making meals that tasted like we were millionaires. Her version of Salisbury steak uses potato chips—not a common addition, but I love the saltiness they add. But Salisbury steak is ultimately about that gravy, and this one is a winner.

PREP TIME: 15 minutes • **COOK TIME:** 30 minutes • **MAKES 4 SERVINGS**

1. **MAKE THE HAMBURGER PATTIES:** In a large bowl, combine the ground beef, eggs, potato chips, ground mustard, garlic powder, salt, and pepper. Using your hands, mix together the ingredients until fully combined. Form into four ½-inch-thick patties, about ¼ pound each.

2. In a 12-inch skillet over medium-high heat, melt the butter in the oil. Fry the patties on both sides, about 5 minutes per side, until cooked through. Remove the patties to a plate lined with paper towels. Pour off any excess grease from the skillet, but do not wipe the skillet clean.

3. **MAKE THE GRAVY:** Reduce the heat to medium and add the sliced onion. Stir and cook until golden brown and somewhat soft, 3 to 5 minutes.

4. In a medium bowl, whisk the broth and cornstarch until smooth. Add the broth mixture and Worcestershire sauce to the onions and simmer until thickened, stirring occasionally, 8 to 10 minutes. If the sauce appears too thick, you can add more broth to thin.

5. Return the cooked hamburger patties to the gravy. Spoon the gravy over the top and let simmer until heated through, about 2 minutes.

6. Serve hot. These are great with the Skins-On Mashed Potatoes (page 111).

7. Leftovers can be stored in an airtight container in the refrigerator for 1 or 2 days.

HAMBURGER PATTIES

1 pound (454 g) ground beef

2 large eggs

1 cup (170 g) smashed potato chips

2 teaspoons ground mustard

2 teaspoons garlic powder

¼ teaspoon kosher salt

¼ teaspoon freshly ground black pepper

1 tablespoon unsalted butter

1 tablespoon olive oil

GRAVY

1 small yellow onion, halved and thinly sliced (about ½ cup / 74 g)

2 cups (480 ml) beef broth, plus more as needed

1 tablespoon cornstarch

1 teaspoon Worcestershire sauce

Kosher salt and freshly ground black pepper

HAMBURGER STROGANOFF

Hamburger stroganoff is the savory version of apple pie. It's made a thousand different ways, and every way is good. It really depends on how you grew up with it, assuming you were lucky enough to be raised on this meat and pasta dish. This is definitely an American version, but one I know folks will enjoy.

PREP TIME: 10 minutes • **COOK TIME:** 30 minutes • **MAKES 8 SERVINGS**

1. In a large saucepan or deep sauté pan over medium heat, melt the butter. Add the onion and garlic and sauté until tender, about 5 minutes. Add the ground beef and cook, breaking it up with a wooden spoon, until no longer pink, about 8 minutes. Stir in the mushrooms, flour, salt, and pepper and cook for 5 minutes. Add the cream of chicken soup and stir to combine. Lower the heat, cover, and simmer for 10 minutes, stirring occasionally. Last, stir in the sour cream, heating through, about 2 minutes.

2. Serve over the cooked egg noodles and, if desired, garnish with the parsley.

3. Leftovers can be stored in an airtight container in the refrigerator for 1 or 2 days.

2 tablespoons unsalted butter

1 small yellow onion, finely diced (½ cup / 74 g)

1 garlic clove, minced

1 pound (454 g) ground beef

1 pound (454 g) baby bella mushrooms, sliced (about 2 cups)

2 tablespoons all-purpose flour

1 teaspoon kosher salt

½ teaspoon freshly ground black pepper

One 10.5-ounce (298 g) can cream of chicken soup

1 cup (230 g) sour cream

12 ounces (340 g) wide egg noodles, cooked al dente

2 tablespoons minced fresh parsley, for garnish (optional)

SURPRISE MEATLOAF

Meatloaf, while delicious, can seem a bit heavy and dense. But when you hide soft-boiled eggs inside, the entire dynamic changes, giving you rich, perfectly seasoned meatloaf with the surprise of light, smooth eggs. It may sound crazy, but the combination works well. Plus, it's super fun to cut into and watch your family's eyes light up!

PREP TIME: 25 minutes • **COOK TIME:** 1 hour 10 minutes • **MAKES 8 SERVINGS**

Nonstick spray

7 or 8 large eggs

1 tablespoon olive oil

2 large yellow onions, finely chopped (about 2 cups / 296 g)

3 pounds (1.4 kg) ground beef

1 cup (70 g) crushed Ritz crackers

3 garlic cloves, minced

2 tablespoons Worcestershire sauce

2 tablespoons kosher salt

2 teaspoons freshly ground black pepper

½ cup (240 ml) whole milk, plus more as needed

Nonstick spray

¼ cup (60 g) ketchup

¼ cup (70 g) sweet barbecue sauce

1. **MAKE THE SOFT-BOILED EGGS:** Bring a pot of water to a boil over medium-high heat (you'll need enough water to cover the eggs by 1 inch). Place 6 of the eggs in the boiling water (you'll need 5 for the meatloaf, but I boil 6 in case one breaks). Cover and let boil for 6 minutes (set a timer; the timing is important).

2. Meanwhile, fill a medium bowl with water and ice.

3. When the eggs are done, use a slotted spoon to remove them to the ice bath. Let sit until cool enough to peel.

4. **PREPARE THE MEATLOAF:** Preheat the oven to 350°F.

5. In a large nonstick skillet, heat the oil over medium-high heat. Add the onions and sauté for 5 to 7 minutes, until softened, stirring frequently. Remove the skillet from the heat and set aside.

6. Carefully peel 5 of the eggs, taking care not to break the whites. (Use the sixth egg if needed.)

7. In a large bowl, combine the ground beef, remaining 2 eggs, crackers, sautéed onions, garlic, Worcestershire sauce, salt, and pepper. Add the milk and mix. The texture should be soft but not runny. Add more milk as needed.

8. Grease a 9 × 13-inch pan with nonstick spray.

9. In the center of the prepared baking dish, use about half the meat mixture to form a 1-inch-thick layer loaf. (The meatloaf will not touch the sides of the pan as it would in a loaf pan.) Form an indentation along the center of the layer and set the soft-boiled eggs in it in a neat row. Carefully place the remaining meat mixture on top of the eggs, sealing the edges around the eggs and pressing the meat in firmly. You will be creating a dome-shaped meatloaf. Remember, the meatloaf should not touch the edges of the pan.

10. In a small bowl, combine the ketchup and barbecue sauce. Mix well and spread over the top of the meatloaf.

11. Bake for 1 hour, or until cooked through to 160°F. Let cool for about 5 minutes and use a baster to get rid of any excess grease from the baking dish before cutting.

12. Leftovers can be stored in an airtight container in the refrigerator for 3 or 4 days.

CREAMY DILL PICKLE BURGER

My favorite summertime food? Burgers. The first *real* day of summer for me is the day we enjoy grilled burgers with my hubby's famous grilled zucchini, seasoned with oil, salt, and pepper. That meal would be my last request should I ever end up on death row. Unless it's winter, in which case I would like meat raffle hot dish. But anyhoo, the shining glory of this burger is that dill pickle topping. *Game changer.* Try it. If you're reading this, it means you're considering making it, and I am here to give you that final nudge. *Do it.*

PREP TIME: 15 minutes • **COOK TIME:** 10 to 15 minutes • **MAKES 4 SERVINGS**

1. In a medium bowl, combine the cream cheese, pickles, ham, ranch seasoning, and green onion. Mix well. Set aside.

2. In a large bowl, combine the ground beef, egg, hamburger seasoning, seasoned salt, kosher salt, and pepper. Mix well.

3. Make four ½-inch-thick patties from the beef mixture, about ¼ pound each.

4. Heat the oil in a large skillet over medium heat. Add the patties and cook for 6 to 8 minutes per side (depending on how well done you like your burger), until cooked through. Flip the patties only one time.

5. Place a burger on the bottom half of each bun and top with a generous amount of the dill pickle topping. Add the top halves of the buns, pressing down to spread the dill pickle mixture.

6. Serve immediately.

One 8-ounce (227 g) package cream cheese

1 cup (154 g) finely diced dill pickles

1 cup (135 g) finely diced deli ham

2 tablespoons Homemade Ranch Seasoning Mix (page 157)

2 tablespoons finely diced green onion

1 pound (454 g) ground beef

1 large egg

2 tablespoons Hamburger Seasoning Mix (page 157)

2 teaspoons seasoned salt

1 teaspoon kosher salt

½ teaspoon freshly ground black pepper

1 tablespoon canola oil

4 hamburger buns, sliced and toasted (optional)

DECONSTRUCTED FRENCH ONION BURGER

If anyone told me I'd be eating a whole onion and *loving it,* I would have called them a liar. But I do make this, and I do love it. If friends are coming over, it's my secret weapon. No one ever expects to be served a stuffed onion, but everyone always gobbles it up!

PREP TIME: 90 minutes • **COOK TIME:** 55 minutes • **MAKES 4 SERVINGS**

4 large (285 g each) sweet onions (about 3 inches in diameter)

¼ cup (½ stick / 57 g) unsalted butter

¼ cup (60 ml) plus 1 tablespoon olive oil

2 teaspoons kosher salt

1 pound (454 g) ground beef, 80/20 blend

1 tablespoon Hamburger Seasoning Mix (page 157)

1 teaspoon garlic powder

½ teaspoon freshly ground black pepper

1 teaspoon Worcestershire sauce

2 cups (226 g) shredded Gruyère cheese

1. Line a sheet pan with parchment paper.

2. Cut about ½ inch off the top and bottom of each onion and remove the outer dry papery layer. Use an apple corer to remove the center of the onion. With clean hands (or carefully using the apple corer), remove the inside layers, leaving 2 outer layers of the onion intact. Reserve the removed inside layers of the onion. (See Note.)

3. Place the hollowed onions on the prepared sheet pan about 1 inch apart.

4. Cut the removed inside onion layers into large dice. This will yield about 8 cups of diced onion.

5. In a large sauté pan over medium-low heat, heat the butter and the ¼ cup oil. Add the diced onions and salt. Cook, uncovered, for 50 to 55 minutes, stirring occasionally. The onions will soften and turn a deep golden brown.

6. **PREPARE THE HAMBURGER:** In a large bowl, combine the ground beef, hamburger seasoning, garlic powder, pepper, and Worcestershire sauce. Mix well.

7. In a large skillet over medium heat, add the beef mixture and cook until the beef is no longer pink, 8 to 10 minutes. Remove from the heat and drain, if necessary. Mix in 1½ cups of the cheese and 1 cup of the caramelized onions.

8. **FILL AND BAKE THE ONIONS:** Preheat the oven to 375°F.

9. Spoon the beef mixture into the center of the hollowed-out onions (about 1 cup per onion). Top with the remaining caramelized onions, so that the stuffed onions are overflowing.

10. Bake for 35 minutes, or until cooked through and the outer onions are soft. Remove the pan from the oven. Top the onions with the remaining ½ cup cheese. Bake for another 10 minutes, or until the cheese is hot and bubbling.

11. Leftovers can be stored in an airtight container in the refrigerator for 1 or 2 days. I recommend reheating in the oven at 375°F for 15 minutes, or until heated through. The onions won't look as pretty after reheating, but they'll still taste good.

NOTE: You can hollow out and slice the onions the day before to save some time when making this dish. Store the onions in a sealed container in the refrigerator up to overnight. You can even stuff the onions ahead of time, cover, and refrigerate.

CRANBERRY WILD RICE MEATBALLS

This wouldn't be a book about midwestern cooking if it didn't include wild rice. It doesn't really get more Minnesota than wild rice and hot dish. Did you know that real wild rice is only grown naturally right here in Minnesota? Despite its name, it's not actually rice at all—it's more like rice's close cousin. It's harvested from the seed of an aquatic plant and is used in a number of dishes, including hot dish, soups, and, of course, meatballs.

PREP TIME: 20 minutes • **COOK TIME:** 25 minutes • **MAKES 30 MEATBALLS, ABOUT 10 SERVINGS**

1. **MAKE THE MEATBALLS:** Preheat the oven to 350°F. Line a sheet pan with parchment paper.

2. In a large bowl, whisk the egg. Add the ground beef, ground sausage, wild rice, cranberries, cheese, parsley, salt, and pepper. Mix until just combined.

3. In a medium bowl, combine the milk, bread crumbs, onion, and garlic. Add the milk mixture to the meat mixture and stir until just combined, taking care not to overwork the ingredients.

4. Wet your clean hands to keep the meat from sticking to them. (I usually rinse and re-wet my hands after every 4 meatballs or so.) Form meatballs using 2 tablespoons of the meat mixture for each. Place them on the prepared sheet pan as you finish.

5. Bake the meatballs for about 25 minutes, until the outsides are browned and they reach an internal temperature of 160°F on a meat thermometer. Transfer to a serving dish.

6. **MAKE THE SAUCE:** Combine the barbecue sauce and jellied cranberries in a medium saucepan. Use a wooden spoon to break up the cranberry sauce. Place the pan over medium-low heat and whisk until the mixture is well combined and heated through. Pour over the meatballs.

7. Serve warm.

8. Leftovers can be stored in an airtight container in the refrigerator for 3 or 4 days.

MEATBALLS

1 large egg

1 pound (454 g) ground beef

1 pound (454 g) ground pork sausage

1 cup wild rice, cooked according to the package directions

½ cup (43 g) dried cranberries

½ cup (50 g) grated Parmesan cheese

2 tablespoons chopped fresh parsley

2 teaspoons kosher salt

½ teaspoon freshly ground black pepper

½ cup (120 ml) milk

½ cup (54 g) fine dry bread crumbs

½ small yellow onion, finely chopped (¼ cup / 37 g)

2 garlic cloves, minced

SAUCE

1 cup (280 g) barbecue sauce

One 14-ounce (397 g) can jellied cranberries

BUFFALO STUFFED CHICKEN

Stuffing things into chicken is such a fun way to live. Make it Buffalo chicken and I am in heaven. Should you happen to be from the Midwest like myself and prefer ranch dressing, have no fear. Just omit the blue cheese.

PREP TIME: 15 minutes • **COOK TIME:** 20 to 25 minutes • **MAKES 4 SERVINGS**

1. Preheat the oven to 350°F. Grease a large oven-safe skillet with nonstick spray.

2. **PREPARE THE CHICKEN:** Season both sides of each chicken breast with the salt and pepper. With a clean hand on top of the chicken breast to keep it in place, use a sharp knife to cut a 2- to 3-inch-deep pocket into the chicken (depending on the size of the breast). Be careful to not slice all the way through the breast. You just want a well for the cream cheese mixture.

3. **MAKE THE BLUE CHEESE FILLING:** In a medium bowl, combine the blue cheese, cream cheese, ranch seasoning, and crumbled bacon.

4. Stuff each chicken pocket with the cream cheese mixture (about 3 tablespoons per chicken breast). Weave a few toothpicks into the open edges of the chicken to secure each pocket.

5. Pour ¼ cup of the Buffalo sauce into the prepared skillet. Place the stuffed chicken breasts on top. Brush ½ cup of the Buffalo sauce over the chicken breasts, covering all the surfaces.

6. Cook for 20 to 25 minutes, until the internal temperature of the thickest part of the chicken reaches 165°F.

7. Serve immediately, topped with the remaining ¼ cup Buffalo sauce and garnish, if desired, with a drizzle of ranch dressing and the diced celery. Season with salt and pepper to taste.

8. Leftovers can be stored in an airtight container in the refrigerator for 1 or 2 days.

CHICKEN

Nonstick spray

4 boneless, skinless chicken breasts (about ½ pound / 227 g each)

¼ teaspoon kosher salt, plus more to taste

¼ teaspoon freshly ground black pepper, plus more to taste

1 cup (260 g) Frank's RedHot Buffalo sauce

BLUE CHEESE FILLING

¼ cup (38 g) crumbled blue cheese

One 8-ounce (227 g) package cream cheese, at room temperature

2½ tablespoons Homemade Ranch Seasoning Mix (page 157)

3 bacon slices, cooked until crisp, then crumbled (about ½ cup / 45 g)

Ranch dressing, for garnish (optional)

1 celery stalk, diced (about ½ cup / 50 g), for garnish (optional)

STUFFED FRENCH ONION CHICKEN

Did I mention I like stuffing things into chicken? This one is a no-brainer. Glorious caramelized onions nestled beautifully inside a perfectly seasoned chicken breast and covered in cheese and gravy? That is one big *heck yes* from me.

PREP TIME: 30 minutes • **COOK TIME:** 45 minutes • **MAKES 4 SERVINGS**

3 tablespoons unsalted butter

2 large yellow onions, halved and thinly sliced (about 2 cups / 296 g)

2¼ cups (540 ml) beef broth

4 boneless, skinless chicken breasts (about 1 pound / 454 g total)

2 tablespoons olive oil

¼ teaspoon kosher salt

¼ teaspoon freshly ground black pepper

¼ teaspoon dried basil

¼ teaspoon dried thyme

8 slices deli provolone cheese

4 slices deli Swiss cheese

2 tablespoons all-purpose flour

1. Preheat the oven to 425°F.

2. In a large oven-safe skillet over medium-high heat, melt the butter. Add the onions and ¼ cup of the broth and cook until the onions are browned and tender, 15 to 20 minutes, stirring often. Transfer the cooked onions to a medium bowl and tent with foil to keep warm. Set the skillet aside to use again.

3. Butterfly each chicken breast. Put the chicken breast on a cutting board and, with a clean hand flat on top of the breast to keep it in place, use a sharp knife to cut into one side of the breast, starting at the thicker end and ending at the thin point. Be careful not to slice all the way through the breast. You should be able to open the chicken like a book.

4. In a small bowl, combine the oil, salt, pepper, basil, and thyme. Rub over the outside and inside of each chicken breast.

5. Open each chicken breast and lay 1 slice provolone cheese, 1 slice Swiss cheese, and 2 tablespoons of the onions on half of the breast. Close the chicken breast and weave a few toothpicks into the open edges of the chicken to secure each pocket.

6. Return the skillet to the stovetop over medium heat. Add the stuffed chicken and cook for 6 to 8 minutes on each side, until the chicken is lightly browned but still a little pink in the middle. Transfer the chicken breasts to a plate and tent with foil to keep warm.

7. Return the remaining onions to the skillet over medium-high heat. Sprinkle the flour on top and stir to coat the onions evenly. Add the remaining 2 cups broth and bring the mixture to a boil, stirring frequently. Return the stuffed chicken breasts to the skillet and top each with one of the remaining 4 provolone slices.

8. Transfer the skillet to the oven and cook for 8 to 10 minutes, until the internal temperature of the chicken is 165°F. The cheese should be melted and bubbly.

9. Spoon some of the gravy over the chicken and serve.

10. Leftovers can be stored in an airtight container in the refrigerator for 1 or 2 days.

CHICKEN ALFREDO WITH BRUSSELS SPROUTS

Brussels sprouts are one of those polarizing foods—people seem to love or hate them. I firmly fall in the love category. Adding their sweet, nutty, smoky flavor to a traditional dish just seemed like a good idea. And it was!

PREP TIME: 45 minutes • **COOK TIME:** 10 minutes • **MAKES 8 SERVINGS**

1. Preheat the oven to 415°F. Line a sheet pan with foil.

2. Lay the bacon strips on the prepared sheet pan. Bake for 18 to 20 minutes, until crispy. Transfer to a plate lined with paper towels to drain and cool, then crumble and set aside.

3. Reduce the oven temperature to 400°F and line a second sheet pan with foil.

4. Spread the Brussels sprouts in a single even layer on the prepared sheet pan. Drizzle with 2 tablespoons of the oil and season with ½ teaspoon of the salt and ¼ teaspoon of the pepper. Cook until light golden brown and tender, 12 to 15 minutes.

5. Meanwhile, prepare the chicken and pasta. Season the chicken with ½ teaspoon each of the remaining salt and pepper. Heat the remaining 1 tablespoon oil in a large skillet over medium heat. Add the chicken and cook until no longer pink, 4 to 5 minutes, and it reaches an internal temperature of 165°F. Place the chicken on a plate and tent with foil to keep warm.

6. In a large saucepan or Dutch oven, melt the butter over medium heat. Add the cream, the remaining 1 teaspoon salt, and the remaining ¼ teaspoon pepper and bring to a slow, rolling boil. Gently boil until the mixture begins to thicken, 3 to 5 minutes. Remove from the heat and stir in the Parmesan. Add the crumbled bacon, Brussels sprouts, chicken, and noodles. Toss to combine. If you find the sauce to be too thick, add more cream to thin. Stir well and serve hot.

7. Leftovers can be stored in an airtight container in the refrigerator for 1 or 2 days.

8 bacon slices

1 pound (454 g) Brussels sprouts, trimmed and halved (or quartered depending on size)

3 tablespoons olive oil

2 teaspoons kosher salt

1 teaspoon freshly ground black pepper

2 boneless, skinless chicken breasts (about 1 pound / 454 g total), cut into 1-inch cubes

2 tablespoons unsalted butter

2 cups (480 ml) heavy cream, plus more as needed

1 cup (100 g) grated Parmesan cheese

1 pound (454 g) fettuccine noodles, cooked al dente

SUN-DRIED TOMATO CHICKEN BITES

Did you know there is an entire movement about eating for your blood type? I did some research and decided to try it for a bit, which meant no to red meat but yes to chicken. As I was eating a *lot* of chicken, I kept trying new ways to enjoy it. This is one of my favorites. Easy, perfectly flavored bites paired with sun-dried tomatoes. What's not to love about sun-dried tomatoes?

PREP TIME: 20 minutes • **COOK TIME:** 25 minutes • **MAKES 6 SERVINGS**

1. Preheat the oven to 425°F.

2. In a small saucepan over medium heat, bring 2 cups (480 ml) water to a boil. Add the sun-dried tomatoes and reduce the heat to low. Simmer for 3 to 4 minutes, until the tomatoes are softened. Drain the water and finely chop the tomatoes. Set aside.

3. In a medium bowl, combine the chicken chunks, salt, pepper, and oil. Toss to coat.

4. Place the chicken in a single layer in a large oven-safe skillet over medium heat. Sear on all sides (about 2 minutes per side), then remove from the heat and set aside.

5. In a small bowl, combine the chopped sun-dried tomatoes, garlic, thyme, red pepper flakes, and heavy cream. Pour the mixture over the chicken.

6. Transfer the skillet to the oven and bake for 12 minutes. Sprinkle evenly with the Gruyère and bake for 6 to 8 minutes more, until the cheese is melted and the chicken is cooked through and has an internal temperature of 165°F.

7. Garnish with the Parmesan and parsley. Serve with toothpicks.

8. Leftovers can be stored in an airtight container in the refrigerator for 1 or 2 days.

½ cup (25 g) sun-dried tomatoes

4 boneless, skinless chicken breasts (about 2 pounds / 908 g total), cut into 1½-inch chunks

½ teaspoon kosher salt

½ teaspoon freshly ground black pepper

1 tablespoon canola oil

2 teaspoons minced garlic

1 teaspoon dried thyme

1 teaspoon crushed red pepper flakes

½ cup (120 ml) heavy cream

1 cup (113 g) shredded Gruyère cheese

¼ cup (25 g) freshly grated Parmesan cheese

Chopped fresh parsley, for garnish

FRENCH ONION PORK CHOPS

I probably shouldn't tell you this, but if I have a choice between steak, chicken, or pork chops, pork chops rank dead last. I think that came from experiencing a dry pork chop in my youth. But when they're smothered in caramelized onions and cheese and perfectly cooked, they are a delicious masterpiece!

PREP TIME: 40 minutes • **COOK TIME:** 12 minutes • **MAKES 5 SERVINGS**

1. Preheat the oven to 425°F.

2. In a large oven-safe skillet over medium-high heat, melt the butter. Add the onions and ½ cup of the broth and cook until the onions are golden brown and tender, 15 to 20 minutes. Transfer to a bowl and tent with foil to keep warm. Do not wipe out the skillet.

3. In a small bowl, combine the oil, salt, pepper, and Italian seasoning. Rub over both sides of the pork chops.

4. Add the seasoned pork chops to the skillet. Cook over medium heat until well browned, 5 to 8 minutes on each side. Remove the pork chops to a plate and set aside. (They don't have to be fully cooked at this point.)

5. In a small bowl, whisk the remaining 1 cup broth and the flour. Return the onions to the skillet, add the broth mixture, and bring to a low boil. Cook until thickened, 5 to 8 minutes. Add the pork chops, including the juices. Top with the cheese.

6. Transfer the skillet to the oven and bake for 8 to 10 minutes, until the cheese is melted.

7. Place the skillet under the broiler and broil until the cheese is hot and bubbly and the internal temperature of the pork is 145°F, 1 to 2 minutes.

8. Spoon some of the onion mixture over the top and serve.

9. Leftovers can be stored in an airtight container in the refrigerator for 1 or 2 days.

3 tablespoons unsalted butter

2 large yellow onions, halved and thinly sliced (about 2 cups / 296 g)

1½ cups (360 ml) beef broth

2 tablespoons olive oil

1 teaspoon kosher salt

¼ teaspoon freshly ground black pepper

1 teaspoon Italian Seasoning (page 156)

Five 1-inch-thick boneless pork chops (about 6.5 ounces / 182 g each)

3 tablespoons all-purpose flour

1 cup (113 g) shredded Gruyère cheese

Chopped fresh parsley, for garnish

CHERRY PORK CHOPS

I am starting to see it now . . . really see how I add a "sweet" element to savory dishes to fine-tune them to my liking. It all started when I was three and was offered candy apple *salad*. The lines were blurred between sweet and savory, and I've never looked back. The cherry sauce in this recipe is one of those easy sauces that makes me feel like a gourmet chef when I prepare it. And yes, it can go on almost any protein!

PREP TIME: 10 minutes • **COOK TIME:** 35 minutes • **MAKES 4 SERVINGS**

1. In a medium saucepan, heat the ½ teaspoon oil over medium heat. Add the shallot and cook until fragrant, about 1 minute. Add the wine and cherry preserves and cook for 12 to 15 minutes, stirring frequently. (It should be a thin syrup.)

2. Meanwhile, season both sides of the pork chops with the salt and pepper.

3. In a large skillet over medium heat, heat the 1 tablespoon oil. Add the pork chops and cook them for 8 to 10 minutes on each side, until a meat thermometer reads 145°F. Remove the chops to a plate and tent with foil to keep warm.

4. Add the cream cheese, broth, Parmesan, and vinegar to the skillet. Whisk until blended and heated through. Return the chops to the pan, right on top of the cream cheese mixture.

5. Plate the pork chops with the cream cheese mixture underneath. Top them with the cherry syrup and serve.

6. Leftovers can be stored in an airtight container in the refrigerator for 1 or 2 days.

1 tablespoon plus ½ teaspoon olive oil

1 medium shallot, minced (about ¼ cup / 40 g)

½ cup (120 ml) dry red wine or beef broth

½ cup (160 g) cherry preserves

Four 1-inch-thick boneless pork chops (about 6 ounces / 170 g each)

½ teaspoon kosher salt

½ teaspoon freshly ground black pepper

One 8-ounce (227 g) package cream cheese, at room temperature, cubed

1 cup (240 ml) chicken broth

¼ cup (25 g) grated Parmesan cheese

¼ cup (64 g) balsamic vinegar

JALAPEÑO POPPER–STUFFED PORK

This beast of a recipe is simply the best. It's my all-time favorite way to enjoy pork loin—the jalapeño popper filling was made for pork. This is a showstopping meal!

PREP TIME: 30 minutes • **COOK TIME:** 1 hour • **MAKES 10 SERVINGS**

1. Preheat the oven to 450°F.

2. Butterfly the pork: Place the pork on a cutting board and, with a clean hand flat on top of the meat, hold a sharp knife parallel to the board and carefully make a lengthwise cut about a third of the way from the bottom, stopping about 1 inch from the opposite end. Be careful not to cut all the way through. Open the loin like a book. Continue the cut, now slicing halfway from the bottom and stopping about 1 inch from the opposite edge. Open that edge as well. You now have one large, evenly flat piece of pork.

3. Cover the entire cut of meat with plastic wrap and use a meat mallet to pound to an even ⅓-inch thickness. Season both sides with the salt and pepper.

4. In a medium bowl, combine the cream cheese, bacon, and ranch seasoning. Spread the cream cheese mixture in an even layer on the pork loin, leaving about a ½-inch border on the edges. Sprinkle 1 cup of the cheddar and the jalapeños evenly over the cream cheese mixture.

5. Tightly roll the pork loin to completely enclose all the fillings. Using kitchen twine, tightly secure the roll.

6. In a large oven-safe skillet over medium heat, heat the olive oil. Add the pork loin and sear, about 5 minutes on all four sides.

7. Transfer the skillet to the oven and roast until the pork loin reaches an internal temperature of 145°F (be sure to insert the thermometer all the way into the center of the loin). Start checking at 25 to 30 minutes, but the loin might need up to 50 minutes.

8. Sprinkle the loin with the remaining 1 cup cheddar and roast for 5 more minutes, or until the cheese is hot and bubbly.

9. Slice and, if desired, garnish with parsley. Serve hot.

10. Leftovers can be stored in an airtight container in the refrigerator for 1 or 2 days.

1 center-cut pork loin (about 3 pounds / 1,361 g)

½ teaspoon kosher salt

½ teaspoon freshly ground black pepper

One 8-ounce (227 g) package cream cheese, at room temperature

10 bacon slices, cooked until crisp, then crumbled (about 1⅔ cups / 150 g)

1 tablespoon Homemade Ranch Seasoning Mix (page 157)

2 cups (226 g) shredded cheddar cheese

2 jalapeño peppers, finely diced (about ⅓ cup / 30 g)

1 tablespoon olive oil

Finely chopped fresh parsley, for garnish (optional)

OVEN PULLED PORK

I love oven-roasted pulled pork because I love pulled pork and I love adding pulled pork to everything. Having a really strong base recipe is important, and this one is just that. When I was working on this recipe, I was testing half a teaspoon versus a whole teaspoon of garlic powder, really wanting to make sure that every measurement was perfect. But at the end of the day, if you measure it with your heart, that will work too.

PREP TIME: 20 minutes • **COOK TIME:** 6½ hours • **MAKES 16 SERVINGS**

1. Preheat the oven to 225°F.

2. Trim any excess fat from the pork. In a small bowl, combine the kosher salt, pepper, paprika, onion powder, garlic powder, ground mustard, chipotle powder, and celery salt. Rub the spices all over the pork.

3. Place the pork in a Dutch oven, cover, and roast for 5½ hours. Remove the lid and roast for 1 more hour. The pork should be very tender, pull apart easily with a fork, and have an internal temperature of 195°F.

4. Remove the pork from the Dutch oven and let rest until cool enough to work with.

5. Shred the pork using two forks. Store in an airtight bag (remove as much air from the bag as possible) in the refrigerator for 3 days or in the freezer for up to 3 months.

4 to 6 pounds (1.8 to 2.7 kg) boneless pork butt, Boston butt, or pork shoulder

2 teaspoons kosher salt

1 teaspoon freshly ground black pepper

1 teaspoon smoked paprika

1 teaspoon onion powder

½ teaspoon garlic powder

½ teaspoon ground mustard

½ teaspoon chipotle powder

½ teaspoon celery salt

NOTE: Extra pulled pork is great on a sandwich! Just add some BBQ sauce and lunch is served!

PULLED PORK MAC AND CHEESE

I love adding pulled pork to things! First off, macaroni and cheese! Creamy, cheesy, glorious macaroni and cheese topped with seasoned pulled pork. You can leave it on top or you can stir it all in as the recipe suggests. Either way, this dish is amazing day 1, day 2, and if you're lucky, even day 3. It's mom-needs-to-rest-grab-some-leftovers dinner perfection!

PREP TIME: 5 minutes • **COOK TIME:** 20 minutes • **MAKES 8 SERVINGS**

1. In a medium bowl, mix together the pulled pork and barbecue sauce. Set aside.

2. Cook the pasta according to the package directions. Drain and set aside.

3. Meanwhile, melt the butter in a saucepan over medium heat. Add the flour and whisk constantly for 1 to 2 minutes, until the mixture turns light brown. Remove from the heat and gradually pour in the warm milk, whisking constantly. Return the pan to the heat and whisk until thickened, 3 to 5 minutes. Add 2½ teaspoons salt, the ground mustard, garlic powder, and, if desired, the cayenne and stir to combine. Remove from the heat. Add the cheeses and stir until melted.

4. Pour the sauce over the cooked pasta. Stir to combine, then taste and season with salt and pepper as needed.

5. If necessary, reheat the pulled pork.

6. Serve the mac and cheese topped with pulled pork and sprinkled with chopped parsley.

7. Leftovers can be stored in an airtight container in the refrigerator for 3 or 4 days. When reheating I will sometimes add 1 to 2 tablespoons of milk to the macaroni and cheese to ensure creaminess.

3 cups (747 g) Oven Pulled Pork (page 151)

½ cup (140 g) barbecue sauce

1 pound (454 g) elbow macaroni

½ cup (1 stick / 113 g) unsalted butter

½ cup (63 g) all-purpose flour

3 cups (720 ml) whole milk, warmed

Kosher salt

½ teaspoon ground mustard

¼ teaspoon garlic powder

¼ teaspoon cayenne pepper (optional)

1 cup (113 g) grated sharp cheddar cheese

½ cup (57 g) grated mozzarella cheese

Freshly ground black pepper

Chopped fresh parsley, for garnish

Seasonings

Having a pantry stocked with homemade seasonings is amazing! When preparing my own seasoning blends, I like to buy the freshest quality herbs and spices I can. They are usually inexpensive and so easy to throw together. And they can really liven up a dish. If you are always looking for homeschooling lessons like I am, you could have your kids measure out the ingredients and fill the jars. Math, dexterity, art—all wrapped up in a spicy bundle. ☺

HAMBURGER SEASONING MIX

ITALIAN SEASONING

TACO SEASONING

HOMEMADE TACO SEASONING

This taco seasoning is the secret to making Skillet Hamburger Nachos (page 65).

PREP TIME: 5 minutes • **MAKES ABOUT ½ CUP**

2 tablespoons chili powder

1 tablespoon ground cumin

2 teaspoons onion powder

2 teaspoons garlic powder

2 teaspoons sea salt

2 teaspoons freshly ground black pepper

1 teaspoon paprika

½ teaspoon dried oregano

½ teaspoon crushed red pepper flakes

Whisk all the ingredients together in a small bowl. Store in an airtight container at room temperature for up to 6 months.

ITALIAN SEASONING

Use this mix for all your Italian-inspired dishes, like Lasagna Soup (page 83), Spaghetti Pizza (page 121), and French Onion Pork Chops (page 145).

PREP TIME: 5 minutes • **MAKES ABOUT ½ CUP**

2 tablespoons dried marjoram

2 tablespoons dried rosemary

2 tablespoons dried oregano

2 tablespoons dried thyme

2 tablespoons dried basil

Whisk all the ingredients together in a small bowl. Store in an airtight container at room temperature for up to 6 months.

HAMBURGER SEASONING MIX

The ultimate burger seasoning! Use it for Mushroom Swiss Sliders (page 52), Cheeseburger Soup (page 84), Cheeseburger Salad (page 95), and more.

PREP TIME: 5 minutes • **MAKES ABOUT ½ CUP**

Whisk all the ingredients together in a small bowl. Store in an airtight container at room temperature for up to 6 months.

- 2 tablespoons paprika
- 2 tablespoons onion flakes
- 2 tablespoons kosher salt
- 4 teaspoons freshly cracked black pepper
- 2 teaspoons garlic powder
- 2 teaspoons granulated sugar
- 2 teaspoons chili powder
- 1 teaspoon crushed red pepper flakes

HOMEMADE RANCH SEASONING MIX

The cornerstone of Midwest cuisine, ranch! Use this mix in Dill Pickle Cheese Ball Bites (page 49), Creamy Dill Pickle Burger (page 131), Buffalo Stuffed Chicken (page 137), and Jalapeño Popper–Stuffed Pork (page 149).

PREP TIME: 5 minutes • **MAKES ABOUT ½ CUP**

Whisk all the ingredients together in a small bowl. For a more finely ground seasoning, pulse the mixture in a food processor to the desired consistency. Store in an airtight container at room temperature for up to 6 months.

NOTE: To use this seasoning for ranch dressing, whisk 1 tablespoon of the seasoning mix with ⅓ cup mayonnaise and ⅓ cup whole milk.

- ⅓ cup (40 g) powdered buttermilk
- 2 tablespoons dried parsley
- 2 teaspoons dried onion flakes
- 2 teaspoons onion powder
- 2 teaspoons garlic powder
- 1½ teaspoons dried dill weed
- 1 teaspoon kosher salt

SIDES

EVERY SINGLE RECIPE in this chapter is extra. (I heard my teenager say that; hope I am using it right.) I wanted to call out one specifically and highlight its awesomeness, but I simply could not choose.

These are hearty sides and not to be misinterpreted as healthy in any way. Even the vegetables. I wrap carrots in bacon, smother Brussels sprouts in a maple-bourbon glaze, and add heavy cream and enormous amounts of butter to mashed potatoes.

In my humble opinion, most folks know how to roast and steam vegetables and I didn't want to take up any precious recipe space with basic options. We aren't basic, we are extra! (I'm definitely using that right. I just know it.) I want you to be just as wowed with the sides as you are with the main dish. And these recipes will absolutely do that!

BALSAMIC ROASTED BRUSSELS SPROUTS

So simple, yet so satisfying. Is there anything that balsamic vinegar doesn't taste good on? I'll never know. This is an easy side dish that complements chicken, steak, pork, and even nonmeat options.

PREP TIME: 10 minutes • **COOK TIME:** 20 to 25 minutes • **MAKES 4 SERVINGS**

1. Preheat the oven to 450°F. Line a sheet pan with foil.

2. In a small bowl, whisk the oil, 1½ tablespoons of the balsamic vinegar, the garlic, salt, and pepper.

3. Spread the sprouts in an even layer on the prepared sheet pan. Drizzle the oil mixture over the sprouts and toss to evenly coat. Spread back into an even layer.

4. Roast for 20 to 25 minutes, until the sprouts are tender with a crisp outside.

5. Drizzle with the remaining 1½ tablespoons vinegar and sprinkle with salt to taste.

6. Leftovers can be stored in an airtight container in the refrigerator for 1 or 2 days.

1½ tablespoons olive oil

3 tablespoons balsamic vinegar

2 garlic cloves, minced

½ teaspoon kosher salt, plus more to taste

¼ teaspoon freshly ground black pepper

1 pound (454 g) fresh Brussels sprouts, trimmed and halved lengthwise

MAPLE-BACON BRUSSELS SPROUTS

Quite possibly the best Brussels sprouts you may ever try. I have to make two batches, because they are gobbled up so quickly around here. Even picky eaters fall in love with these!

PREP TIME: 15 minutes • **COOK TIME:** 35 minutes • **MAKES 8 SERVINGS**

1. Preheat the oven to 425°F. Line a sheet pan with foil.

2. Place the Brussels sprouts on the prepared sheet pan. Drizzle with the oil and sprinkle with the salt and pepper. Toss to combine. Spread the Brussels sprouts into an even layer.

3. Bake for 20 to 25 minutes, until crispy, turning halfway through.

4. Meanwhile, in a large skillet over medium-high heat, cook the bacon until crispy, 7 to 8 minutes. Remove the bacon bits to a plate lined with paper towels to drain. Set aside.

5. Remove the skillet from the heat and add the bourbon and balsamic vinegar to the skillet. Immediately return the skillet to medium-high heat, scrape up the browned bits from the pan, and stir to combine. Bring the bourbon to a boil and add the maple syrup and brown sugar, stirring constantly until the sauce begins to thicken, 10 to 12 minutes.

6. Remove from the heat and add the cooked Brussels sprouts, bacon, and candied pecans. Toss to combine and serve.

2 pounds (908 g) Brussels sprouts, trimmed and halved lengthwise

2 tablespoons olive oil

¼ teaspoon kosher salt

¼ teaspoon freshly ground black pepper

4 bacon slices, finely diced (about ⅔ cup / 62 g)

2 ounces (¼ cup / 60 ml) bourbon

1 tablespoon balsamic vinegar

½ cup (120 ml) pure maple syrup

½ cup (100 g) packed light brown sugar

½ cup (65 g) chopped candied pecans

BACON-WRAPPED CARROTS

This three-ingredient recipe is how I got my carrot-hating daughter to try cooked carrots. She did initially protest but ultimately gave in and took the tiniest of bites. We were rewarded with a small smile as she admitted it "wasn't that bad." Which means *so amazing* in my book.

PREP TIME: 15 minutes • **COOK TIME:** 35 minutes • **MAKES 8 SERVINGS**

1. Preheat the oven to 425°F. Line a sheet pan with parchment or aluminum foil.

2. Lay the bacon slices on the prepared pan and bake for about 10 minutes, until cooked but not yet crispy. Remove the bacon to a plate lined with paper towels to drain and cool slightly.

3. Reduce the oven temperature to 400°F.

4. Starting at the thick end of one carrot, wrap 1 slice of bacon around it, taking care not to overlap the bacon layers. Repeat to wrap the rest of the carrots. Arrange the carrots on a wire rack on a parchment or foil-lined sheet pan.

5. Bake for 20 to 25 minutes, until the bacon is crispy and the carrots are tender.

6. Remove the pan from the oven and use a pastry brush to carefully glaze all sides of the carrots with the maple syrup. Bake for 5 more minutes, or until the syrup is heated through.

7. Serve hot.

8. Leftovers can be stored in an airtight container in the refrigerator for 1 or 2 days.

1 pound (454 g) bacon (not thick-cut)

2 pounds (908 g) small carrots (less than ½ inch thick)

¼ cup (60 ml) pure maple syrup

HOMESTYLE CREAMED CORN

Nothing makes me feel more homesteady than creamed corn. Well, that and my ceramic jar of wooden spoons. That's weird to admit, but true. Standing over the range stirring corn and watching it thicken is my happy place. Wrong, eating this is my happy place. Okay, they both are.

PREP TIME: 10 minutes • **COOK TIME:** 20 minutes • **MAKES 8 SERVINGS**

1. Preheat the oven to 400°F.

2. In a large oven-safe skillet over medium heat, combine the corn, cream, butter, sugar, salt, and pepper.

3. In a small bowl, whisk the milk and flour. Pour into the corn mixture. Continue to cook over medium heat, stirring occasionally, until the liquid starts to thicken, 10 to 12 minutes. Top with the Parmesan cheese.

4. Bake in the oven for 5 to 8 minutes, until the cheese is melted.

5. Garnish with the basil, if desired, and serve.

One 16-ounce (454 g) package frozen corn kernels, thawed

1 cup (240 ml) heavy cream

2 tablespoons unsalted butter

2 tablespoons granulated sugar

2 teaspoons kosher salt

½ teaspoon freshly ground black pepper

½ cup (120 ml) whole milk

3 tablespoons all-purpose flour

¼ cup (25 g) grated Parmesan cheese

1 teaspoon finely chopped fresh basil, for garnish (optional)

HUNDRED-CLOVE MASHED POTATOES

The sweet roasted garlic flavor in these potatoes makes them full of creamy, wake-up-your-taste-buds deliciousness. The garlic flavor is not overpowering in the slightest (I promise!), and it's just special enough to make your mashed potatoes the best on the block.

PREP TIME: 1 hour • **COOK TIME:** 25 minutes • **MAKES 12 SERVINGS**

1. Preheat the oven to 400°F. Line a pie pan with foil.

2. Peel and discard the papery outer layer of the garlic bulb. Keep the bulb intact. (Do not detach the individual garlic cloves.) Cut off the top ½ inch of the garlic bulb, just enough to expose the cloves. Place the garlic heads cut side up in the prepared pan. Drizzle with the oil, letting the oil soak in around the cloves. Top with another sheet of foil and seal the edge of the pan.

3. Bake for 45 to 55 minutes, until the garlic cloves are soft and deep golden brown. Set aside to cool.

4. Meanwhile, place the potatoes in a large pot and cover with salted water. Cover the pot and bring to a boil over medium-high heat. Boil, uncovered, until fork-tender, about 25 minutes. Drain the potatoes and return them to the pot off the heat.

5. Lightly mash the potatoes. Add the butter and cream and mash to your desired consistency of creaminess.

6. Squeeze all the garlic cloves into a medium bowl. Discard the remaining skin. Mash the garlic until smooth. This should be about 1 cup (280 g) of roasted garlic cloves. Add to the potatoes and mix well.

7. Season to taste with salt and pepper.

8. Leftovers can be stored in an airtight container in the refrigerator for 3 or 4 days.

8 large heads of garlic, about 100 cloves

3 tablespoons olive oil

6 pounds (2.7 kg) red potatoes, washed and cut into 2-inch chunks

1 cup (2 sticks / 227 g) unsalted butter, at room temperature

1 cup (120 ml) heavy cream

Kosher salt

Freshly ground black pepper

TOMATO PIE

If you happen to love tomatoes, this is a fantastic use for them. Nothing beats a fresh BLT with warm tomatoes straight from the garden, but this is a close second. You can use store-bought pie crust, but if you want to make it the best ever, use my recipe for the ideal flaky crust. If possible, let the tomatoes dry for the full time listed—you don't want tomato pie soup.

PREP TIME: 30 minutes • **DRYING TIME:** 24 hours • **COOK TIME:** 35 to 40 minutes • **MAKES 8 SERVINGS**

1. Lay the sliced tomatoes in a single layer on one or more sheet pans lined with paper towels. Sprinkle the tomatoes with 1 teaspoon of the salt and let sit at room temperature for 24 hours (or 1 hour at minimum). This time allows the paper towels to absorb the excess liquid drawn out of the tomatoes by the salt. (If you are leaving them out for longer than 1 hour, you can cover with paper towels as well for an extra layer of absorption.)

2. When you're ready to make the pie, preheat the oven to 350°F.

3. On a lightly floured surface, roll out the homemade pie crust and place it in a 9-inch pie pan. Press the pie crust securely against the pie pan, taking care to secure the edge of the crust to the rim of the pie pan. (If you're using an unrolled packaged crust, roll it out to flatten it slightly before placing it in the pan.)

4. In a medium bowl, combine the mozzarella, cheddar, Parmesan, mayonnaise, oregano, garlic powder, the remaining 1 teaspoon salt, the black pepper, and cayenne. Scoop half the cheese mixture into the pie shell and spread to cover the bottom. Add half the bacon, half the green onions, and half the basil. Layer with half the sliced tomatoes. Scoop and spread out the remaining cheese mixture. Top with the remaining bacon, green onions, and basil and a final layer of tomatoes.

5. Bake for 35 to 40 minutes, until the crust is browned.

6. Cool slightly, then cut into slices and serve warm.

7. Leftovers can be stored in an airtight container in the refrigerator for 1 or 2 days.

5 large heirloom tomatoes (910 g), cored and cut into ¼-inch-thick slices

2 teaspoons kosher salt

Flour, for rolling out the dough

½ recipe (one 9-inch) unbaked Never-Fail Pie Crust (page 239) or store-bought pie crust

1½ cups (170 g) grated mozzarella cheese

1½ cups (170 g) grated cheddar cheese

¼ cup (25 g) grated Parmesan cheese

1½ cups (348 g) mayonnaise

1½ teaspoons dried oregano

1 teaspoon garlic powder

1 teaspoon freshly ground black pepper

½ teaspoon cayenne pepper

6 bacon slices, cooked until crisp, then cut into bite-size pieces (about 1 cup / 91 g)

4 green onions, finely chopped (about ½ cup / 50 g)

10 fresh basil leaves, finely chopped

CHERRY CHICKEN PASTA

Dried cherries are the star of this chicken pasta show. They add texture and a pop of flavor that round out this dish beautifully. I usually serve this at barbecues or in warmer months, but it's hearty enough to serve all year long.

PREP TIME: 15 minutes • **MAKES 8 SERVINGS**

1. In a large bowl, combine the chicken, cooked pasta, red onion, and dried cherries.

2. In a medium bowl, combine the mayonnaise, poppyseed dressing, salt, and pepper.

3. In a large dry skillet over medium heat, toast the almonds until golden, 3 to 4 minutes, stirring often and watching carefully so they don't burn. Transfer to a small plate to cool.

4. Fold the dressing mixture and toasted almonds into the chicken mixture.

5. Top with the green onions, if desired, and serve immediately at room temperature (see Note).

NOTE: If you're not ready to serve immediately, reserve the toasted almonds. Chill the pasta and fold in the almonds just before you serve.

2 cups (280 g) shredded rotisserie chicken

1 pound (454 g) gemelli or rotini pasta, cooked al dente

1 small red onion, finely chopped (about ½ cup / 74 g)

5 ounces (141 g) dried cherries

1 cup (232 g) mayonnaise

1 cup (141 g) Homemade Poppyseed Dressing (recipe follows)

1 teaspoon kosher salt, or to taste

¼ teaspoon freshly ground black pepper, or to taste

½ cup (54 g) slivered almonds

1 tablespoon chopped green onions, for garnish (optional)

Homemade Poppyseed Dressing

PREP TIME: 5 minutes • **MAKES 1½ CUPS**

1. Combine all the ingredients in a medium bowl. Blend with an immersion blender until smooth, about 30 seconds.

2. Store leftover dressing in an airtight container in the refrigerator for up to 1 week.

½ cup (120 ml) vegetable oil

⅓ cup (67 g) granulated sugar

½ cup (120 ml) white vinegar

2 tablespoons mayonnaise

1 tablespoon Dijon mustard

1 teaspoon kosher salt

1 teaspoon finely grated yellow onion

1 tablespoon poppy seeds

ROASTED POTATO SALAD

Potato salad is a tradition, a staple, a classic dish that inspires loyalty and dedication in the hearts of memaws around the country. Everyone thinks their recipe is the best, and usually they're right. The main difference in my recipe is that I roast the potatoes ahead of time instead of just boiling them. It adds a depth of flavor that will have you going back for seconds! If you're scared of trying something new when it comes to potato salad, try roasting the potatoes following my directions and then use them in your regular potato salad recipe!

PREP TIME: 15 minutes • **COOK TIME:** 45 to 60 minutes • **MAKES 8 SERVINGS**

1. Preheat the oven to 425°F. Line a sheet pan with foil or parchment paper.

2. **MAKE THE POTATOES:** Spread the potatoes on the prepared sheet pan and sprinkle them with the kosher salt, seasoned salt, and pepper. Drizzle the oil on top and use your clean hands to toss the potatoes, making sure every piece is coated.

3. Bake for 45 to 60 minutes, until the potatoes are crispy. Turn once halfway through baking.

4. Let the potatoes cool for at least 15 minutes.

5. **ASSEMBLE THE SALAD:** In a large bowl, combine the roasted potatoes, red onion, bacon, eggs, mayonnaise, mustard, dill, and pepper. (You can reserve 1 or 2 eggs for garnish if you like.) Using a spatula, gently fold the ingredients until fully combined.

6. Serve warm or refrigerate in an airtight container until ready to serve. If desired, garnish with chopped green onion before serving.

7. Leftovers can be stored in an airtight container in the refrigerator for 3 or 4 days.

POTATOES

3 pounds (1.4 kg) red potatoes, washed and cut into small cubes

1 teaspoon kosher salt

1 teaspoon seasoned salt

1 teaspoon freshly ground black pepper

2 tablespoons olive oil

SALAD

1 medium red onion, finely diced (about ⅔ cup / 98 g)

8 bacon slices, cooked until crisp, then crumbled (about 1¼ cups / 124 g)

6 large eggs, hard-boiled and roughly chopped

1 cup (232 g) mayonnaise

1 tablespoon yellow mustard

¼ teaspoon dried dill

¼ teaspoon freshly ground black pepper

1 tablespoon chopped green onions, for garnish (optional)

ZUCCHINI

THERE IS A KNOWN PHRASE in rural Minnesota, "Don't leave your cars unlocked at night. You might find a stack of zucchini on your front seat in the morning."

Why such an ominous threat? Zucchini grows prolifically. And if you're a gardener, you can't bear to see any of the fruits of your harvest wasted, so you offer it up to friends and strangers alike.

The beauty and joy of zucchini is that it can be used in almost any dish. It can replace meat, makes a fabulous noodle, can be used as a terrific crust for pizza, and adds moisture to baked goods without changing the flavor of the dessert.

If you have never baked or cooked with zucchini, this is your sign to try it. Start with a baked good, like Zucchini Brownies, and work up to the Five-Cheese Zucchini Crust Pizza. If you are already a fan of cooking with zucchini, I know you'll be delighted with how amazing these recipes turn out!

To say that it is my favorite fruit to work with is an understatement. (And yes, it is technically a fruit; folks just commonly use it as a vegetable.) I'm obsessed! Clearly. I hope by the end of this chapter you'll be obsessed too!

SKILLET ZUCCHINI ZOODLES

I don't do many trends or fads, but this one is worth it. I love zoodles—not because they are healthy but because they taste so good! This is one of my favorite ways to enjoy them, smothered in cheese. These are great on their own but also served with a nice grilled steak.

PREP TIME: 25 minutes • **COOK TIME:** 10 minutes • **MAKES 6 SERVINGS**

1. Rinse the zucchini well in cool or lukewarm water and trim off both ends to create a flat surface. Spiralize the zucchini (see Note). Trim the zoodles to 6 to 8 inches, or about the length of a spaghetti noodle.

2. In a large skillet over medium-high heat, heat 2 tablespoons of the olive oil. Add the zoodles. Stir until cooked through, about 6 minutes. Place in a strainer to drain any excess liquid. Set aside.

3. Mix together the Parmesan, salt, and pepper in a small bowl. Set aside.

4. In the same skillet you cooked the zoodles in, heat the remaining 1 tablespoon oil over medium-low heat. Add the garlic and sauté for 1 minute. Add the heavy cream, stir in the cheese mixture, and cook for 2 to 3 minutes to melt the cheese. Add the zoodles and toss them in the sauce until coated and heated through.

5. Plate and serve immediately.

NOTE: Here are a few ways to make zoodles:

- Julienne peeler
- Mandoline
- Spiralizer attachment to a stand mixer
- Handheld spiralizer

Or you can purchase them in the produce department of your grocery store.

2 or 3 medium zucchini (1,782 g)

3 tablespoons olive oil

1½ cups (150 g) finely grated Parmesan cheese

1 teaspoon kosher salt

1 teaspoon freshly ground black pepper

1 tablespoon minced garlic

½ cup (120 ml) heavy cream

ZUCCHINI CORN CHOWDER

This soup is hearty and filling and would be super healthy, except I add cream and bacon. Whoops! But the cream and bacon help to make an extra velvety soup with just the right amount of salty bacon deliciousness.

PREP TIME: 10 minutes • **COOK TIME:** 30 minutes • **MAKES 8 SERVINGS**

1. In a large heavy-bottom stockpot or Dutch oven over medium heat, melt the butter. Add the bacon and cook until the bacon renders its fat and begins to brown, 3 to 4 minutes. Add the onion, garlic, and thyme and cook over medium heat, stirring a couple of times, until the vegetables begin to soften, about 5 minutes. Add the potatoes and broth, increase the heat to medium-high, and bring to a simmer. Lower the heat to medium and simmer, uncovered, for 8 to 10 minutes, until the potatoes are halfway cooked. Add the zucchini, corn, 1 teaspoon of the jalapeños, and the half-and-half. Stir in the salt and pepper and simmer until the vegetables are completely tender, 8 to 12 minutes.

2. Using a ladle, remove about half the chowder to a large bowl. Puree the chowder remaining in the pot with an immersion blender until smooth. Return the unprocessed chowder to the pot and stir. (If you do not have an immersion blender, use a regular blender, taking care to fill it no more than halfway full. Be sure not to burn yourself!)

3. Season with more salt and pepper to taste.

4. Serve garnished with chopped parsley, the remaining jalapeños, and, if desired, a sprinkle of cayenne.

5. Leftovers can be stored in an airtight container in the refrigerator for 3 or 4 days.

1 tablespoon unsalted butter

2 bacon slices, roughly chopped

½ large yellow onion, finely chopped (about 1 cup / 126 g)

2 garlic cloves, minced

½ teaspoon dried thyme

1 pound (454 g) russet potatoes, peeled and cut into ½-inch dice

4 cups (960 ml) chicken broth

1 medium zucchini, cut into ½-inch dice (about 1½ cups / 210 g)

2¾ cups (437 g) fresh corn kernels (from about 4 ears)

2 teaspoons diced jalapeño pepper

1 cup (240 ml) half-and-half or heavy cream

⅛ teaspoon kosher salt, plus more to taste

⅛ teaspoon freshly ground black pepper, plus more to taste

Chopped fresh parsley, for garnish

Cayenne pepper (optional)

FIVE-CHEESE ZUCCHINI CRUST PIZZA

I honestly can't sing the praises of this zucchini pizza crust highly enough. It's so flavorful and crispy—and the perfect way to use up some of that zucchini! And let's talk about this cheese sauce: Five different cheeses come together beautifully and will probably blow your mind with their rich decadence. This tastes like a gourmet pizza!

PREP TIME: 20 minutes • **COOK TIME:** 55 minutes • **MAKES 8 SERVINGS**

1. Preheat the oven to 400°F.

2. **MAKE THE ZUCCHINI CRUST:** Rinse the zucchini and trim off the ends. Shred the zucchini with a fine grater. Gently wrap the shredded zucchini in paper towels or a clean towel and squeeze to remove any excess water.

3. In a large bowl, combine the zucchini, onion, garlic, mozzarella, eggs, flour, salt, pepper, and the 2 teaspoons oil. Mix well and let sit for about 5 minutes. Mix again.

4. Spread the 2 tablespoons oil evenly in a 12-inch oven-proof skillet. Add the zucchini mixture and spread it out evenly as well.

5. Bake for 35 minutes, or until the crust is golden brown. Do not turn off the oven.

6. Remove the skillet from the oven and loosen the crust from the edges of the pan. Use two spatulas to flip the crust in the skillet (or invert a plate over the skillet, flip the skillet to release the crust, and slide the crust back into the skillet upside down).

7. Bake for another 10 minutes, or until browned. Do not turn off the oven—the pizza will go in one last time.

8. **MAKE THE CHEESE SAUCE:** In a medium bowl, combine the ricotta, mozzarella, Parmesan, Romano, cream cheese, garlic, salt, pepper, and parsley. Mix together well and set aside.

(continued)

ZUCCHINI CRUST

1 extra-large zucchini (grated and drained, about 4 cups)

½ small white or yellow onion, finely grated and drained (about ½ cup / 74 g)

1 teaspoon minced garlic

½ cup (57 g) shredded mozzarella cheese

2 large eggs, whisked

2 cups (250 g) all-purpose flour

1 teaspoon kosher salt

½ teaspoon freshly ground black pepper

2 tablespoons plus 2 teaspoons olive oil

CHEESE SAUCE

½ cup (123 g) ricotta cheese

¼ cup (28 g) shredded mozzarella cheese

¼ cup (25 g) finely grated Parmesan cheese

¼ cup (25 g) finely grated Romano cheese

3 ounces (⅓ cup / 85 g) cream cheese, at room temperature

1 teaspoon minced garlic

½ teaspoon kosher salt

¼ teaspoon freshly ground black pepper

1 teaspoon minced fresh parsley

10 grape or cherry tomatoes, halved lengthwise
(about 1 cup / 170 g)

3 or 4 basil leaves, cut into thin strips

9. **ASSEMBLE THE PIZZA:** It's time to put everything together! With the crust still in the skillet, spread the cheese mixture evenly on top (leaving a ½-inch border). Top with the grape tomatoes and basil.

10. Return to the oven and bake until the toppings are browned, 10 to 12 minutes.

11. Remove from the oven, slice, and serve hot.

TIPS FOR BAKING WITH
ZUCCHINI

- **SIZE MATTERS.** A large zucchini will be drier; a small zucchini will have more moisture. Certain recipes work better when you use the size specified.

- **YOU DO NOT NEED** to peel zucchini. It really depends on how you want your finished product to look. If you want the zucchini to hide out in the recipe and be your little secret, simply peel it and it will disappear into the other ingredients. If you happen to like the small flecks of green and want folks to know what they're getting, don't peel the zucchini. But do wash it well first.

- **USE THE FINE SIDE** of a grater when grating zucchini. Coarser pieces will have a slightly more noticeable flavor and texture in a finished cake or bread recipe.

- **SOME RECIPES DIRECT THAT** you press zucchini well with a clean towel to soak up excess moisture and to keep whatever you're baking from getting too soggy. Pay close attention to the recipe instructions, as the level of moisture the zucchini provides is important. For instance, in Zucchini Brownies (page 195), the zucchini is the main source of moisture and should *not* be drained!

CHOCOLATE ZUCCHINI CAKE

Amazingly rich and decadent, this cake is what all chocolate cakes should strive to be, and it's so easy to make. No one will notice the zucchini in the cake, but they'll be happy it's there as soon as they take a bite and see how moist this cake is! I have paired it with chocolate buttercream, but truthfully, this cake is fantastic all on its own!

PREP TIME: 25 minutes • **COOK TIME:** 40 to 50 minutes • **MAKES 15 SERVINGS**

1. Preheat the oven to 350°F. Grease a 9 × 13-inch baking dish with nonstick spray.

2. In a medium bowl, use a spatula to stir together the sugar, eggs, oil, and vanilla. Add the flour, cocoa powder, baking soda, and baking powder. Mix well. Fold in the zucchini until evenly distributed. Pour the mixture into the prepared baking dish.

3. Bake for 40 to 50 minutes. The cake is done when an inserted toothpick comes out with a few crumbs but no wet batter clinging to it.

4. Let the cake cool to room temperature. Then spread the cake with the frosting, slice, and serve.

Nonstick spray

2 cups (400 g) granulated sugar

4 large eggs, at room temperature

1½ cups (360 ml) vegetable oil

1 teaspoon vanilla extract

2 cups (250 g) all-purpose flour

¾ cup (95 g) unsweetened cocoa powder

2 teaspoons baking soda

1 teaspoon baking powder

3 cups (450 g) grated zucchini, undrained (from 2 or 3 medium zucchini)

Chocolate Buttercream (page 250)

WHITE ZUCCHINI CAKE WITH ROASTED STRAWBERRY SAUCE

Let me tell you a few things about this cake. It is moist. Literally one of the moistest white cakes I have ever made. The crumb is tender. It is delicate yet flavorful. Then it is paired with a homemade roasted strawberry sauce. This cake is the definition of summer!

See photo on page 190.

PREP TIME: 30 minutes • **COOK TIME:** 25 to 30 minutes • **MAKES 8 SERVINGS**

Nonstick spray

½ cup (1 stick / 113 g) unsalted butter, at room temperature

⅔ cup (133 g) granulated sugar

½ teaspoon vanilla extract

4 large (124 g) egg whites, at room temperature

2 cups (250 g) sifted all-purpose flour

2 tablespoons cornstarch

1 tablespoon baking powder

¼ teaspoon kosher salt

⅔ cup (160 ml) whole milk

1 small zucchini, peeled and finely shredded, undrained (about 1 cup / 150 g)

Roasted Strawberry Sauce (recipe follows)

Whipped cream, for serving (optional)

1. Preheat the oven to 350°F. Grease a 9-inch Bundt pan with nonstick spray.

2. In the bowl of a stand mixer fitted with the paddle attachment or in a large bowl using a handheld mixer, combine the butter, sugar, and vanilla. Mix on medium speed for 30 seconds, then mix on high for 2 to 4 minutes. The mixture should be light and fluffy. Add the egg whites and mix on medium until just incorporated.

3. In a medium bowl, sift together the flour, cornstarch, baking powder, and salt.

4. Add about a third of the flour mixture to the creamed butter and sugar, mixing on low to combine. Gradually mix in half the milk, another third of the flour mixture, then the remaining milk and flour mixture. Continue mixing on low until just combined. Fold in the shredded zucchini and its liquid by hand.

5. Pour the batter into the prepared pan and bake for 25 to 30 minutes. The cake is done when a toothpick inserted into the center comes out with a few crumbs but no wet batter clinging to it. You do not want to overbake this cake.

6. Let the cake cool in the pan for 15 minutes, then invert it onto a large serving plate.

7. To serve, pour the strawberry sauce over the whole cake, reserving some for serving individual slices. Top each slice of cake with a dollop of whipped cream, if desired, and a drizzle of strawberry sauce.

Roasted Strawberry Sauce

PREP TIME: 10 minutes • **COOK TIME:** 10 to 12 minutes • **MAKES 3 CUPS**

1. Preheat the oven to 400°F. Line a sheet pan with parchment paper.

2. Place the strawberry slices in a single layer on the prepared sheet pan and drizzle them evenly with the maple syrup. Sprinkle the cinnamon on top.

3. Roast for 10 to 12 minutes, until the berries are tender and have begun to release their juices.

4. Combine the strawberry preserves and roasted strawberries in a medium bowl and mix with a fork. If you prefer a thinner syrup, add up to ½ cup warm water.

2 cups (144 g) sliced fresh strawberries

2 tablespoons pure maple syrup

¼ teaspoon ground cinnamon

One 10-ounce (283 g) jar strawberry preserves

WHITE ZUCCHINI CAKE WITH ROASTED STRAWBERRY SAUCE, PAGE 188

ZUCHINNI CAKE WITH CREAM CHEESE FROSTING, PAGE 192

ZUCCHINI CAKE WITH CREAM CHEESE FROSTING

This is like a tender spice cake. As a matter of fact, you'd never know there's zucchini in this cake if not for the green bits. I've tried this recipe with chopped nuts and fruit and have even served it without frosting. (Then it's okay to eat for breakfast.) But speaking of frosting, this is my tried-and-true cream cheese frosting. Once you try it, you may never need another. Total cake perfection!

See the photo on page 191.

PREP TIME: 35 minutes • **COOK TIME:** 1 hour 5 minutes • **MAKES 15 SERVINGS**

Nonstick spray

1 cup (200 g) granulated sugar

1 cup (200 g) packed light brown sugar

2 teaspoons ground cinnamon

¼ teaspoon ground nutmeg

1¼ cups (300 ml) vegetable oil

2 teaspoons vanilla extract

4 large eggs

3¼ cups (406 g) all-purpose flour

2 teaspoons baking soda

½ teaspoon baking powder

1 teaspoon kosher salt

3 cups (450 g) grated zucchini, undrained (from 2 or 3 medium zucchini)

Cream Cheese Frosting (recipe follows)

1. Preheat the oven to 350°F. Grease a 9 × 13-inch baking pan with nonstick spray.

2. In a large bowl, combine the granulated sugar, brown sugar, cinnamon, and nutmeg. Mix until smooth. Add the oil and mix until incorporated. Mix in the vanilla, then the eggs, one at a time, whisking to incorporate after each addition.

3. In a medium bowl, whisk the flour, baking soda, baking powder, and salt. Add the dry ingredients to the wet ingredients and beat with a hand mixer on medium until combined. Use a spatula to gently fold in the grated zucchini.

4. Pour the batter into the prepared pan.

5. Bake for 60 to 65 minutes. The cake is done when an inserted toothpick comes out with a few crumbs but no wet batter clinging to it.

6. Let cool completely.

7. Use an offset spatula to spread the frosting on top of the cooled cake. Cut the cake and serve.

Cream Cheese Frosting

PREP TIME: 5 minutes • **MAKES ENOUGH TO COVER A 9 X 13-INCH CAKE**

In a large bowl, beat the cream cheese with a hand mixer on medium until creamy. Add the butter and beat on medium until combined. Add the confectioners' sugar, milk, and vanilla and beat on low until the sugar is mostly worked in. Turn the mixer to medium and beat until the sugar is fully incorporated.

4 ounces (114 g) cream cheese, at room temperature

8 tablespoons (1 stick / 114 g) unsalted butter, at room temperature

2 cups (250 g) confectioners' sugar

1½ tablespoons whole milk

½ teaspoon vanilla extract

ZUCCHINI BROWNIES

When I first made these zucchini brownies in 2012, I declared that I would never need another brownie recipe. That was silly, because you can never have enough brownie recipes and having a stockpile of really good brownie recipes is essential. But these are simply that good. They happen to not use eggs, should you have an allergy or know someone who is avoiding them.

PREP TIME: 10 minutes • **COOK TIME:** 25 to 35 minutes • **MAKES 12 BROWNIES**

1. Preheat the oven to 350°F. Grease a 9 × 13-inch baking pan with nonstick spray and line with parchment paper on the bottom and up the sides for easy brownie removal.

2. In a large bowl, combine the oil, sugar, and vanilla and stir until fully incorporated. Add the flour, cocoa powder, baking soda, and salt and mix until combined. The batter will be very dry at this point. Fold in the zucchini by hand.

3. Let the batter rest for 5 minutes. Add the chocolate chunks and stir. The batter should appear more wet. If not, let it rest for 5 more minutes and stir again.

4. Spread the brownie mixture evenly in the pan and bake for 25 to 35 minutes. The brownies are done when a toothpick inserted into the center comes out with a few crumbs but no wet batter clinging to it.

5. Let the brownies cool in the pan for about 10 minutes, then cut and serve.

6. Leftovers can be stored in an airtight container at room temperature for 3 or 4 days.

Nonstick spray

½ cup (120 ml) vegetable oil

1½ cups (300 g) granulated sugar

1 tablespoon vanilla extract

2 cups (250 g) all-purpose flour

½ cup (64 g) unsweetened cocoa powder

1½ teaspoons baking soda

1 teaspoon kosher salt

3 cups (450 g) finely shredded zucchini, undrained (from 2 to 3 medium zucchini)

1¼ cups (210 g) semi-sweet chocolate chunks

NOTE: In this recipe, the zucchini is the main source of moisture, so it should not be drained.

COOKIES, BARS, AND DESSERTS

THIS IS THE longest chapter in the book, but did you expect anything else from me? Desserts have been my passion and driving force for a decade now, and any recipe included in this book has been vigorously tested and absolutely perfected—that I guarantee.

If you are looking for a good Minnesota dessert, try the Marshmallow Scotcheroo Bar. I kicked these Special K bars up a notch by adding marshmallow fluff, a very midwestern thing to do. It's also the main ingredient in our salads. A salad frosting, if you will.

This chapter has all the things—cakes, cookies, bars (a midwestern staple), and even chocolate bread (which in itself is not very sweet but when made into an ooey-gooey marshmallow pull-apart bread becomes quite a showstopper).

As the saying goes, "*Stressed* spelled backward is *desserts*!" After you try one of these recipes, may you be blessed with a stress-free sweet treat that will be a new staple in your house.

DECORATING
SUGAR COOKIES

These cookies are amazing on their own but definitely shine when you introduce a decorating element. When it comes to decorating sugar cookies, the sky's the limit. I often use a basic glaze recipe that is also known as "easy royal icing," even though there is no meringue powder added.

- 1 cup (125 g) confectioners' sugar
- 1 tablespoon milk
- 1 tablespoon light corn syrup
- Drop of lemon juice
- Food coloring (optional)

IN A SMALL BOWL, mix the confectioners' sugar, milk, corn syrup, and lemon juice until smooth. Add food coloring, if desired, and pipe or spread onto cookies.

While this glaze tastes amazing and often looks beautiful if you take the time to pipe intricate designs, it does require specific tools and supplies. Folks usually want a variety of food colors, and that means making a big batch, adding it to dozens of bowls, using piping bags and specific tips for every color, learning piping and flooding techniques, and so on. (I could write a book on this type of cookie decorating—it's a passion of mine!)

However, the vast majority of folks want an easy and delicious option that everyone can do. My solution? Buttercream. Just use the recipe from my White Cake with Whipped Vanilla Buttercream (page 241). It accepts color beautifully, so you can make colorful themed cookies! No piping bags needed, just a knife. Place a dollop of frosting on each cookie and spread in an even layer. They are delicious to eat as is, but you can also add sprinkles, candies, or even another cookie to make a sandwich cookie.

SUGAR COOKIES

If you're looking for a fantastic cut-out cookie recipe, this is the one for you. My secret is the almond extract, which does magical things to sugar cookie dough. I have been shouting it from the rooftops for a decade now, so it might not be a secret anymore. Nonetheless! These cookies never disappoint.

PREP TIME: 15 minutes • **BAKE TIME:** 6 to 8 minutes • **MAKES 15 COOKIES**

1. In the bowl of a stand mixer fitted with the paddle attachment or in a large bowl using a handheld mixer, cream the butter and sugar on high speed until well combined, about 2 minutes. With the mixer on low, add the eggs and egg yolks, mixing until well incorporated. Turn off the mixer and scrape the sides of the bowl. With the mixer back on low, add the vanilla and almond extracts and mix until incorporated.

2. Sift together the flour, salt, and baking powder into a medium bowl. With the mixer running on medium-low speed, combine the flour mixture with the butter mixture about a cup at a time until fully incorporated.

3. Wrap the dough in plastic wrap and refrigerate for at least 1 hour and up to overnight.

4. When ready to bake, preheat the oven to 350°F. Line a sheet pan with parchment paper.

5. Roll the dough out on a floured surface to ¼- to ½-inch thick. Cut out the dough into your desired shapes. Place on the prepared sheet pan about 1 inch apart. These cookies do not spread very much.

6. Bake for 6 to 8 minutes, watching the cookies carefully so the edges don't burn.

7. Let the cookies rest for about 10 minutes on the sheet pan, then transfer them to a wire rack to cool completely. Have fun decorating!

8. Store leftover cookies in an airtight container at room temperature.

1½ cups (3 sticks / 339 g) unsalted butter, at room temperature

2 cups (400 g) granulated sugar

2 large eggs, at room temperature

2 large egg yolks

1 tablespoon vanilla extract

2 teaspoons almond extract

4 cups (500 g) all-purpose flour, plus more for rolling out the dough

1 teaspoon kosher salt

1 teaspoon baking powder

SNICKERDOODLES

I tested these cookies for *months* and I'm not kidding you; they really are perfect. If you want a soft snickerdoodle, this is the recipe for you!

PREP TIME: 15 minutes • **BAKE TIME:** 6 to 8 minutes • **MAKES 54 COOKIES**

1. Preheat the oven to 375°F. Line three sheet pans with parchment paper.

2. In the bowl of a stand mixer on high or in a large bowl using a handheld mixer, cream the butter and the 1½ cups sugar on high speed until lighter in color and fully combined, 2 to 3 minutes. Add the eggs, one at a time, then add the vanilla, mixing until fully incorporated. With the mixer on low, add the flour, cream of tartar, baking soda, and salt. Mix until fully incorporated.

3. Using a fork or a small whisk, mix together the 3 tablespoons sugar and the cinnamon in a large shallow bowl.

4. Use a 1-tablespoon scoop to form rounded cookie dough balls. Roll each one in the cinnamon sugar. Place 2 inches apart on the prepared sheet pans. They do not need to be flattened.

5. Bake for 6 to 8 minutes, until the cookies have risen and no longer appear wet in the center.

6. Immediately, carefully transfer the cookies to a rack to cool. They will deflate slightly.

7. Store leftover cookies in an airtight container at room temperature.

1 cup (2 sticks / 227 g) unsalted butter, at room temperature

1½ cups (300 g) plus 3 tablespoons granulated sugar

2 large eggs, at room temperature

1 tablespoon vanilla extract

2¾ cups (344 g) all-purpose flour

1 teaspoon cream of tartar

1 teaspoon baking soda

¼ teaspoon kosher salt

1 tablespoon ground cinnamon

GINGER COOKIES

I was a redhead until about the age of eighteen when I decided to color my hair blond. I hated being called a ginger, and I hated red hair! It never grew in red again—which sounds weird, I know. I really miss it now, and no salon can ever replicate what it was. Also, I really like these ginger cookies.

PREP TIME: 15 minutes • **BAKE TIME:** 10 minutes • **MAKES ABOUT 18 COOKIES**

1. Preheat the oven to 350°F. Line a sheet pan with parchment paper.

2. Sift together the flour, ginger, baking soda, cinnamon, cloves, and salt into a medium bowl. Set aside.

3. In a large bowl, mix together the butter and brown sugar with a handheld mixer on high speed until light and fluffy, 1 to 2 minutes. Add in the egg, combine fully, then stir in the molasses by hand. Add the flour mixture to the molasses mixture and mix on medium speed until fully combined.

4. Place the granulated sugar in a large shallow bowl. Use your clean hands to shape the dough into 2-inch balls and roll them in the granulated sugar. Place the balls 2 inches apart on the prepared sheet pan and flatten them slightly.

5. Bake for 10 minutes, or until the cookies have started cracking on top. The edges may darken slightly.

6. Let the cookies rest for about 5 minutes on the sheet pan, then transfer them to a wire rack to cool completely.

7. Store leftover cookies in an airtight container at room temperature.

2¼ cups (281 g) all-purpose flour

2 teaspoons ground ginger

2 teaspoons baking soda

1 teaspoon ground cinnamon

½ teaspoon ground cloves

¼ teaspoon kosher salt

¾ cup (1½ sticks / 170 g) unsalted butter, at room temperature

1 cup (200 g) packed dark brown sugar

1 large egg, at room temperature

¼ cup (84 g) molasses

¼ cup (50 g) granulated sugar, for rolling

PEANUT BUTTER BLOSSOMS

I included this recipe because it's tried and true and delicious but, most important, because it's traditional. Where I'm from, it just isn't the holidays without these nutty treats. I hope my kids are making these for me when I'm old and gray!

PREP TIME: 5 minutes • **BAKE TIME:** 8 to 10 minutes • **MAKES ABOUT 64 COOKIES**

1. Preheat the oven to 375°F.

2. In the bowl of a stand mixer fitted with the paddle attachment or in a large bowl using a handheld mixer, beat the ½ cup granulated sugar, the brown sugar, peanut butter, butter, and eggs on medium speed until combined. Add the flour, baking soda, and baking powder. Mix until just combined.

3. Place the 2 tablespoons granulated sugar in a large shallow bowl. Use a 1-tablespoon cookie scoop to form rounded cookie dough balls, and roll each one in the sugar. Place 2 inches apart on ungreased sheet pans.

4. Bake for 8 to 10 minutes, until the edges are light brown.

5. Remove from the oven and immediately press a Hershey's Kiss or chocolate star in the center of each cookie.

6. Let the cookies rest for about 5 minutes on the sheet pan, then transfer them to a wire rack to cool completely.

7. Store leftover cookies in an airtight container at room temperature.

½ cup (100 g) plus 2 tablespoons granulated sugar

1 cup (200 g) packed light brown sugar

1 cup (250 g) creamy peanut butter

1 cup (2 sticks / 227 g) salted butter, at room temperature

2 large eggs, at room temperature

3 cups (375 g) all-purpose flour

1½ teaspoons baking soda

1 teaspoon baking powder

One 12-ounce (340 g) bag milk chocolate Hershey's Kisses (or chocolate stars)

BAKING WITH
YOUR KIDS

Baking with your kids is a gift that keeps on giving. Not only does it allow you to spend precious time with them, but it also teaches them skills that they will use well into adulthood. They learn math, reading, timing, and the importance of following directions. And I can usually persuade them to do chores faster with the promise of fresh baked cookies.

Here is the best part of baking with your kids: Eventually they become so good at it that you can say, "Please make me some Snickerdoodles," and they will. Dessert on demand!

As a side note, I would like to offer this up to any future spouses of my children: You're welcome. My boys will enter into marriage with a healthy understanding of not only how to make brownies but also when to make brownies. (Spoiler: There is never a bad time.) And my girls just might acquire spouses based on their crispy-bacon-cooking ability alone.

TOM AND JERRY

I don't know where this drink got its name, nor do I know if the iconic Tom and Jerry bowl with matching cups can even be purchased, but I do know that this is the epitome of a traditional holiday cocktail in Minnesota. This drink is similar to eggnog but *so much better*. I have fond memories of old plastic butter containers with this batter in every grandma's refrigerator. I mean, I didn't drink it then, but I knew it was there. When I finally did get to drink it, I understood completely what all the fuss was about. Belly-warming deliciousness!

PREP TIME: 10 minutes • **MAKES 12 DRINKS**

1. **MAKE THE BATTER:** In a large bowl, beat the egg whites with a hand mixer on medium-high until stiff peaks have formed, about 5 minutes. Set aside.

2. In a small bowl, beat the egg yolks until light and creamy, 1 to 2 minutes.

3. In a large bowl, cream the butter and sugar until no lumps are left and you have a creamy texture. Add the egg whites, egg yolks, vanilla, nutmeg, and cloves. Fold together until well mixed.

4. **MAKE A TOM AND JERRY:** Place ¼ cup of the batter in a mug. Add the brandy and fill the mug with boiling water. Whisk to combine; the drink will become frothy.

5. Serve hot. Store the remaining batter in an airtight container in the refrigerator for 5 to 7 days.

BATTER

6 eggs, yolks and whites separated

8 tablespoons (1 stick / 114 g) unsalted butter

4 cups (500 g) confectioners' sugar

½ teaspoon vanilla extract

½ teaspoon ground nutmeg

½ teaspoon ground cloves

SINGLE TOM AND JERRY COCKTAIL

¼ cup batter

1 ounce (30 ml) brandy

Boiling water

OATMEAL RAISIN COOKIES WITH BOURBON RAISINS

Congratulations! You're actually interested in this recipe and stopped to read all about it. For the last thirty years I've heard this crazy conspiracy that raisin cookies are nowhere near as good as chocolate chip. While chocolate chip cookies will always reign, I happen to love oatmeal raisin, but especially those with bourbon-soaked raisins. These cookies are soft, chewy, and oh so flavorful. Yes, you can omit the bourbon. But because soaking the raisins is an important step, try your favorite spiced tea as a good substitute soaking liquid.

PREP TIME: 10 minutes • **CHILLING TIME:** 30 minutes • **BAKE TIME:** 9 to 11 minutes •
MAKES ABOUT 21 COOKIES

1. Pour the bourbon into a small microwave-safe bowl. Microwave for 1 minute. Add the raisins. Set aside for 30 minutes so the raisins can plump up with bourbon.

2. In the bowl of a stand mixer fitted with the paddle attachment or in a large bowl using a handheld mixer, cream the butter and both sugars on high speed until fully incorporated and fluffy, 2 to 3 minutes. Add the eggs and vanilla and mix until combined. Turn off the mixer and add the flour, oats, baking soda, and cinnamon. With the mixer on low, mix until just combined. Pour the excess bourbon off the raisins and stir the raisins into the cookie dough.

3. Use a 1½-tablespoon cookie scoop to drop portions of the dough 2 inches apart onto an ungreased sheet pan.

4. Place the sheet pan in the refrigerator for 30 minutes or, if covered, up to overnight.

5. When you are ready to bake the cookies, preheat the oven to 350°F.

6. Bake for 9 to 11 minutes, until the edges are lightly golden. The tops of the cookies may appear a little wet, but they will continue to bake out of the oven.

7. Let the cookies rest for about 10 minutes on the sheet pan, then transfer them to a wire rack to cool completely.

8. Store leftover cookies in an airtight container at room temperature.

¾ cup (180 ml) bourbon

1 cup (155 g) raisins

1 cup (2 sticks / 227 g) salted butter, at room temperature

1 cup (200 g) packed light brown sugar

½ cup (100 g) granulated sugar

2 large eggs, at room temperature

1 teaspoon vanilla extract

1½ cups (188 g) all-purpose flour

3 cups (270 g) old-fashioned rolled oats

1 teaspoon baking soda

2 teaspoons ground cinnamon

PECAN SANDIES

Up until about five years ago, I refused to eat any food that had pecans in it. "Yuck!" I'd say in disgust. I wish someone would have slapped me upside the head, because I needed some sense knocked into me. I now crave these buttery, crispy, nutty cookies all year long.

PREP TIME: 20 minutes • **BAKE TIME:** 9 to 11 minutes • **MAKES ABOUT 14 COOKIES**

1. Preheat the oven to 375°F. Line two sheet pans with parchment paper.

2. In the bowl of a stand mixer fitted with the paddle attachment or in a large bowl using a handheld mixer, cream the butter, granulated sugar, and confectioners' sugar on high speed until smooth, 2 to 3 minutes. Add the egg and vanilla and beat until completely incorporated, scraping down the sides of the bowl as necessary. Add the flour, baking powder, and salt to the bowl and mix until just combined. Add the pecans and stir until fully incorporated.

3. Use a 3-tablespoon cookie scoop to drop portions of the dough 2 inches apart onto the prepared sheet pans.

4. Press the bottom of a water glass onto a damp paper towel, then dip it into granulated sugar. Press the glass down onto a dough ball until the dough is about ½ inch thick. Repeat with all the cookies.

5. Bake for 9 to 11 minutes, until the tops of the cookies look dry and the edges are light golden brown.

6. Let the cookies rest for about 5 minutes on the sheet pan, then transfer them to a wire rack to cool completely.

7. Store leftover cookies in an airtight container at room temperature.

1 cup (2 sticks / 227 g) unsalted butter, at room temperature

½ cup (100 g) granulated sugar, plus additional for pressing

½ cup (63 g) confectioners' sugar

1 large egg, at room temperature

1 teaspoon vanilla extract

2 cups (250 g) all-purpose flour, sifted

1 teaspoon baking powder

¾ teaspoon kosher salt

1 cup (109 g) finely chopped pecans

CHEX COOKIES

We call these "ugly cookies." The kids literally ask for them by that name. But what they're lacking in beauty, they make up for in sweetness! This is my favorite cookie to make when someone requests that "i am baker" bring a treat to an event. I set the bar low with looks and wow them with taste. Plus, they are fast and easy, and that's always a bonus in my book.

PREP TIME: 10 minutes • **COOLING TIME:** 30 minutes • **MAKES ABOUT 36 COOKIES**

1. Line two sheet pans with parchment paper. Set aside.

2. In a large saucepan, combine the sugar, corn syrup, and vanilla. Bring to a low boil over low heat, stirring frequently. Carefully add the peanut butter and salt and stir until the peanut butter is melted and fully incorporated. Remove the saucepan from the heat. Add the cereal and stir well, making sure each piece is coated. Stir in the marshmallows until just evenly dispersed. You don't want the marshmallows to melt completely.

3. Use a 2-tablespoon cookie scoop to scoop out mounds of the Chex mixture onto the sheet pans. The cookies do not spread much, so you can place them close together. Let sit for about 30 minutes on the sheet pan to firm up.

4. Store leftover cookies in an airtight container at room temperature, separating layers with wax or parchment paper so the cookies don't stick together.

1 cup (200 g) granulated sugar

1 cup (340 g) light corn syrup

1 teaspoon vanilla extract

1½ cups (375 g) creamy peanut butter

Pinch of kosher salt

5 cups (155 g) Rice Chex cereal

2 cups (100 g) mini marshmallows

BROWNIE COOKIES

I did something a little different with my brownie cookies—I added actual brownie to them. It's a fantastic juxtaposition of chewy and crispy in cookies enhanced with so much chocolate they will make a die-hard chocolate lover swoon.

See the photo on pages 218–219.

PREP TIME: 20 minutes • **BAKE TIME:** 30 minutes • **BROWNIE COOLING TIME:** 30 minutes •
MAKES ABOUT 36 COOKIES

BROWNIE LAYER

Nonstick spray

½ cup (1 stick / 114 g) unsalted butter

1 cup (200 g) granulated sugar

½ cup (75 g) all-purpose flour

⅓ cup (40 g) unsweetened cocoa powder

¼ teaspoon baking powder

¼ teaspoon kosher salt

2 large eggs, at room temperature

1 teaspoon vanilla extract

CHOCOLATE COOKIE LAYER

2½ cups (313 g) all-purpose flour

½ cup (64 g) unsweetened cocoa powder

2 teaspoons cornstarch

1 teaspoon baking soda

½ teaspoon kosher salt

1 cup (2 sticks / 227 g) cold unsalted butter, cut into cubes

1 cup (200 g) packed light brown sugar

½ cup (100 g) granulated sugar

2 large eggs, at room temperature

1½ cups (252 g) semi-sweet mini chocolate chips

1. Preheat the oven to 350°F. Grease a 9 × 13-inch baking dish with nonstick spray.

2. **MAKE THE BROWNIE LAYER:** Melt the butter in a small saucepan or in the microwave and set aside to cool.

3. In a medium bowl, sift together the granulated sugar, flour, cocoa powder, baking powder, and salt.

4. In a large bowl, mix the eggs with the vanilla. Gently add the dry ingredients and stir until combined. Pour the cooled butter into the brownie mixture and mix until just incorporated.

5. Spread the batter in the prepared pan and bake for 15 to 20 minutes. Use a toothpick to test the brownies at 15 minutes; they will be thin. If a few crumbs remain on the toothpick but there is no wet batter, the brownies are done.

6. Set aside to cool for 30 minutes but keep the oven on.

7. **MAKE THE CHOCOLATE COOKIE LAYER:** Line 3 sheet pans with parchment paper.

8. In a medium bowl, sift together the flour, cocoa powder, cornstarch, baking soda, and salt. Set aside. Don't skip the sift!

9. In the bowl of a stand mixer fitted with the paddle attachment or in a large bowl using a handheld mixer, cream the butter and both sugars on high speed until incorporated, 2 to 3 minutes. There may be some small butter cubes remaining, and that is okay. Add the eggs, one at a time, and mix until incorporated. With the mixer on low, add in the sifted dry ingredients and mix until combined, about 30 seconds. The dough will be thick. Remove the bowl from the stand mixer and fold in ½ cup of the semi-sweet chocolate chips.

10. Flip the cooled brownies onto a cutting board and cut off the hard edges on all sides and discard (or have a little snack!).

11. Cut the brownies into small bite-size pieces. I find that ½-inch square is the perfect size. Fold the brownie pieces into the batter. (I use about three-quarters of the brownies, 4 cups total.)

12. Place the remaining 1 cup mini chocolate chips in a large shallow bowl. Use a 2-tablespoon cookie scoop to form rounded cookie dough balls. Dunk a dough ball into the mini chocolate chips. Press it into the bowl to flatten it and fully cover one side of the cookie with the mini chocolate chips. Place the cookie on the sheet pan and repeat with the remaining dough balls. You should be able to fit 8 on one sheet, as the cookies do not spread too much.

13. Bake for 8 to 10 minutes (see Note). Let the cookies rest for about 5 minutes on the sheet pan, then transfer them to a wire rack to cool completely.

14. Store leftover cookies in an airtight container at room temperature.

NOTE: I recommend testing your first batch of cookies for doneness. I tend to take them out of my oven at 8 minutes and then let them cool on the sheet pan to taste-test before I put in the next batch.

BROWNIE COOKIES, PAGE 216

MARSHMALLOW SCOTCHEROO BARS

It simply isn't a get-together without Scotcheroo Bars, also called Special K bars. I take mine a step further and add a layer of marshmallow fluff, because if there's an opportunity to add marshmallow to anything, I'll take it. These are super messy, ooey-gooey, and seriously delightful.

PREP TIME: 15 minutes • **COOLING TIME:** 10 minutes • **MAKES 12 BARS**

1. Line the sides and bottom of a 9 × 13-inch baking dish with parchment paper.

2. In a large saucepan, combine the sugar and corn syrup and bring to a boil over medium heat. Stir in the peanut butter until melted and smooth. Remove from the heat and fold in the cereal until combined.

3. Pat the cereal mixture into an even layer in the prepared baking dish. While the cereal is still warm, spread the marshmallow fluff on top. Let sit for a few minutes to cool and harden.

4. Meanwhile, place the chocolate chips and butterscotch chips in a small microwave-safe bowl. Microwave for 20-second intervals, stirring in between, until smooth—no lumps. Pour over the marshmallow fluff and smooth evenly with a knife.

5. Let the bars cool for about 10 minutes, then cut into 12 bars and serve.

6. Store leftover bars in an airtight container at room temperature for 3 or 4 days.

1½ cups (300 g) granulated sugar

1½ cups (512 g) light corn syrup

1½ cups (387 g) creamy peanut butter

6 cups (186 g) Special K cereal

One 7-ounce (198 g) jar marshmallow fluff

1 cup (170 g) milk chocolate chips

1 cup (170 g) butterscotch chips

LEMON BARS

This amazing lemon bar recipe has two important things: the perfect amount of lemon and a rich buttery crust. I add a bit more lemon juice than most, but it's what sets my lemon bars apart!

PREP TIME: 10 minutes • **BAKE TIME:** 40 minutes • **CHILLING TIME:** 2 hours • **MAKES 12 BARS**

1. Preheat the oven to 350°F. Line the bottom and two sides of a 9 × 13-inch baking dish with parchment paper.

2. **MAKE THE CRUST:** Using a pastry cutter, a fork, or your clean hands, mix together the butter, flour, and granulated sugar in a medium bowl. Press into the bottom of the prepared baking dish.

3. Bake for 15 to 20 minutes, until the edges are golden and the crust is no longer shiny.

4. **MAKE THE FILLING:** In a medium bowl, whisk the granulated sugar and flour. Crack the eggs into a separate medium bowl, then whisk them into the sugar and flour mixture. Add the lemon juice. Pour over the hot baked crust.

5. Return the baking dish to the oven. Bake for 20 minutes, or until the filling is set but not browned.

6. Let the bars cool at room temperature until no longer hot to the touch, 15 to 20 minutes. Refrigerate the bars for at least 2 hours.

7. Dust with confectioners' sugar, cut into squares, and serve.

8. Store leftover bars in an airtight container in the refrigerator for 3 or 4 days.

CRUST

1 cup (2 sticks / 227 g) unsalted butter, at room temperature

2 cups (250 g) all-purpose flour

½ cup (100 g) granulated sugar

FILLING

1½ cups (300 g) granulated sugar

¼ cup (31 g) all-purpose flour

4 large eggs, at room temperature

⅔ cup (160 ml) freshly squeezed lemon juice (from 2 to 3 large lemons)

Confectioners' sugar, for dusting

BUTTERSCOTCH BARS

These bars are peanut butter and butterscotch heaven! They're a mash-up of scotcheroos, Rice Krispies bars, and peanut butter cookies. And making them is as fun as eating them!

You may notice that I say this recipe makes 24 bars instead of 12, even though it is made in a 9 x 13-inch pan. I do that because they are *sweet*. Starting small is a good thing. You can always have two!

These bars chill overnight, so be mindful of that when planning.

PREP TIME: 10 minutes • **BAKE TIME:** 22 minutes • **CHILLING TIME:** 8 to 12 hours • **MAKES 24 BARS**

1. Preheat the oven to 350°F. Line a 9 × 13-inch baking dish with parchment paper on the bottom and up the sides.

2. In a medium bowl, combine the peanut butter, sugar, and egg. Mix well. Spread the peanut butter mixture evenly in the prepared baking dish.

3. Bake for 14 to 15 minutes. Sprinkle evenly with the mini marshmallows. Bake for another 7 minutes, or until the marshmallows are slightly puffy.

4. Meanwhile, in a large pot over medium heat, melt the butterscotch chips, butter, corn syrup, and vanilla. Remove the pot from the heat, add the cereal, and fold it in until combined.

5. Top the marshmallows with the cereal mixture, pressing down to spread it out evenly.

6. Let cool overnight, then cut into 24 bars and serve.

7. Store leftover bars in an airtight container at room temperature for 3 or 4 days.

1 cup (258 g) creamy peanut butter

1 cup (200 g) granulated sugar

1 large egg, at room temperature

One 10-ounce (283 g) package mini marshmallows

One 11-ounce (312 g) package butterscotch chips

¼ cup (½ stick / 57 g) unsalted butter

⅔ cup (227 g) light corn syrup

1 tablespoon vanilla extract

5 cups (145 g) crispy rice cereal

GARBAGE BARS

I'm pretty sure the rest of the world calls these seven-layer magic bars, but I've never been good at doing what everyone else does. Plus, I giggle when my kids ask me for "garbage bars." It's just more fun! We call them garbage bars because they use up all the half-open bags of chips in the pantry that may otherwise have been headed to the garbage. The recipe is so forgiving you can easily switch up flavors and use whatever is hanging out in your pantry!

PREP TIME: 10 minutes • **BAKE TIME:** 30 to 35 minutes • **MAKES 12 BARS**

1. Preheat the oven to 350°F. Line the bottom and two sides of a 9 × 13-inch baking dish with parchment paper.

2. In a medium bowl, mix together the butter and graham cracker crumbs. You want every crumb coated in the butter, as the butter will be the glue that holds the crumb base together.

3. Pour the graham cracker crumbs into the prepared baking dish. Starting at the center and working out to the sides, press the crumbs into a flat layer, then use the bottom of a water glass to press the crust even flatter.

4. Evenly sprinkle the peanut butter chips, milk chocolate chips, white chocolate chips, and butterscotch chips over the graham cracker crust. Evenly drizzle the sweetened condensed milk over the chips. Sprinkle with the coconut.

5. Bake for 30 to 35 minutes, until the edges are browned and the center is mostly set. Let cool for at least 5 minutes, then cut into 12 bars and serve.

6. Store leftover bars in an airtight container at room temperature for 3 or 4 days.

½ cup (1 stick / 114 g) unsalted butter, melted

1½ cups (126 g) graham cracker crumbs

½ cup (84 g) peanut butter chips

½ cup (84 g) milk chocolate or semi-sweet chocolate chips

½ cup (84 g) white chocolate chips

½ cup (84 g) butterscotch chips

Four 14-ounce (1,584 g total) cans sweetened condensed milk

1 cup (93 g) sweetened coconut flakes or shredded coconut

APPLE CARAMEL BARS

There are so many fabulous things happening in this bar—apples, caramel, cheesecake, and a perfect crispy crust. It's like a decadent apple pie, with a little less fuss!

PREP TIME: 20 minutes • **BAKE TIME:** 1 hour 5 minutes • **CHILLING TIME:** 4 to 12 hours •
MAKES 12 BARS

Nonstick spray

CRUST

1 cup (90 g) quick-cooking oats

3 cups (375 g) all-purpose flour

2 cups (400 g) packed light brown sugar

½ teaspoon baking powder

½ teaspoon baking soda

2 teaspoons ground cinnamon

1½ cups (3 sticks / 341 g) unsalted butter, melted

CARAMEL SAUCE

1 cup (200 g) packed light brown sugar

4 tablespoons (½ stick / 57 g) unsalted butter

¼ cup (60 ml) whole milk

1 teaspoon vanilla extract (optional)

CREAM CHEESE MIXTURE

Two 8-ounce (454 g total) packages cream cheese, at room temperature

½ cup (100 g) granulated sugar

1 teaspoon vanilla extract

2 large eggs, at room temperature

1. Preheat the oven to 350°F. Grease a 9 × 13-inch baking dish with nonstick spray.

2. **MAKE THE CRUST:** In a large bowl, combine the oats, flour, brown sugar, baking powder, baking soda, and cinnamon. Pour the melted butter over the mixture and mix together until crumbly. Measure out 2 cups of the mixture and reserve it for the topping.

3. Pour the remaining mixture into the prepared baking dish. Press firmly and evenly into the bottom of the pan.

4. Bake for 18 to 20 minutes, until golden brown.

5. **MAKE THE CARAMEL SAUCE:** Meanwhile, in a medium saucepan, bring the brown sugar, butter, and milk to a gentle boil over medium heat. Cook until thickened, 1 to 2 minutes. Remove from the heat. Mix in the vanilla, if desired, and set aside to cool.

6. **MAKE THE CREAM CHEESE MIXTURE:** In a large bowl, combine the cream cheese, granulated sugar, and vanilla. Mix with a hand mixer on medium speed until smooth and creamy. Turn the mixer to low and beat in the eggs, one at a time, until fully incorporated. Add the caramel sauce (you can reserve a little caramel sauce to drizzle over the bars when serving if you wish). Mix until smooth and fully incorporated. Set aside.

7. **MAKE THE APPLE MIXTURE:** In a large bowl, combine the apples, flour, brown sugar, and cinnamon.

8. **BAKE THE BARS:** Arrange the apples evenly over the baked crust. Spread the cream cheese mixture over the apples. Crumble the reserved oat mixture over the top.

9. Bake for 40 to 45 minutes.

10. Refrigerate the bars for at least 4 hours and up to overnight, then cut into 12 bars. If you reserved any caramel sauce for serving, reheat it and drizzle over the bars just before serving.

11. Store leftover bars in an airtight container in the refrigerator for 3 or 4 days.

APPLE MIXTURE

4 large Granny Smith apples, peeled, cored, and thinly sliced

2 tablespoons all-purpose flour

2 tablespoons light brown sugar

1 teaspoon ground cinnamon

CARAMEL CHOCOLATE CHIP COOKIE BARS

My mother-in-law served these to me fifteen years ago when I was dating my husband. Oddly enough, I had never had one before. I immediately became obsessed with them and started playing around with the recipe, using my favorite chocolate chip cookie recipe as well as a simple yet smooth caramel recipe. It's now perfect, and I can't wait for other folks to have that same "first" moment with them that I did. And hopefully love them as much as I do!

PREP TIME: 10 minutes • **BAKE TIME:** 25 minutes • **MAKES 12 BARS**

CHOCOLATE CHIP COOKIE BARS

1 cup (2 sticks / 227 g) unsalted butter, at room temperature

1½ cups (300 g) packed light brown sugar

1 teaspoon vanilla extract

2 large eggs, at room temperature

2¼ cups (281 g) all-purpose flour

1 teaspoon baking soda

1 teaspoon kosher salt

2 cups (340 g) semi-sweet chocolate chips

CARAMEL SAUCE

One 11-ounce (312 g) package caramel bits or individually wrapped caramels (unwrap them if using)

One 5-ounce (147 ml) can evaporated milk

1. Preheat the oven to 350°F. Line the bottom and two sides of an 8 × 12-inch or 9 × 13-inch baking dish with parchment paper.

2. **MAKE THE BARS:** In a large bowl, cream the butter, brown sugar, and vanilla with a hand mixer until light and fluffy, 2 to 3 minutes. Add the eggs, one at a time, mixing well after each addition. Add the flour, baking soda, and salt and mix on low until combined. Stir in the chocolate chips.

3. Press half the cookie dough into an even layer in the prepared baking dish. Set the remaining cookie dough aside.

4. Bake for 10 minutes.

5. **MAKE THE CARAMEL SAUCE:** Meanwhile, in a medium saucepan over medium heat, melt the caramel in the evaporated milk, stirring frequently until smooth, about 8 minutes. Remove the saucepan from the heat.

6. Place the pan of cookie bars on a heat-safe surface. Carefully pour the hot caramel sauce evenly over the bars, making sure to get it into every nook and cranny.

7. Carefully place flattened dollops of the remaining cookie dough over the hot caramel. I find it works best to pick up a small handful, flatten it in your hand a bit, and place it directly on top of the caramel. Do this with all remaining cookie dough. It's okay if there is some caramel showing between the dollops.

8. Bake for 15 to 18 minutes, until the caramel is bubbling and the cookie dollops are golden brown.

9. Let cool to room temperature, then cut into 12 bars and serve. (See Note for another way to serve.)

10. Store leftover bars in an airtight container at room temperature for 3 or 4 days.

NOTE: We often enjoy these hot—right out of the oven—with ice cream. Reserve some of the caramel sauce you've made. Use a spoon to scoop out a portion of the bars from the pan (it will be ooey-gooey and falling apart—this is a good thing) and place into a bowl. Top with ice cream and the reserved caramel sauce and serve.

HOMEMADE SNICKERDOODLE CRISPY BARS

I have added so many things to Rice Krispies bars—cookies, candy, frostings, you name it. This is by far the best combination. The sweetness from the crispy rice cereal is amplified by the subtle spices in the snickerdoodle. And my Snickerdoodles (page 201) just happen to be soft, so the textures work beautifully together. A winning treat!

PREP TIME: 15 minutes • **MAKES 12 BARS**

1. Grease a 9 × 13-inch baking pan with nonstick spray.

2. In a large saucepan over low heat, melt the butter. Add the large marshmallows and stir until completely melted, 4 to 5 minutes. Remove from the heat. Add the cereal and 2 cups of the chopped cookies. Stir until the cereal is well coated.

3. Scoop half the cereal mixture into the prepared pan. With a clean hand, press down slightly just to get the mixture somewhat even in the pan. Sprinkle the remaining 1 cup cookies in an even layer over the cereal mixture and press them down lightly. Cover with the remaining cereal mixture and press flat with your clean hand. Sprinkle the mini marshmallows over the top and gently press them into the bars.

4. Let cool, cut into 12 bars, and serve.

5. Store leftover bars in an airtight container at room temperature for 3 or 4 days.

Nonstick spray

½ cup (1 stick / 114 g) unsalted butter

One 10-ounce (283 g) bag large marshmallows or 4 cups (200 g) mini marshmallows

4 cups (116 g) Rice Krispies cereal

3 cups roughly chopped Snickerdoodles (page 201) (about 10 cookies)

2 cups (100 g) mini marshmallows, for topping

APPLE CHEDDAR GALETTE

Adding cheese to apple desserts is a magical thing! It's a decades-old concept—one that folks over forty will recognize immediately. I decided to make this one a tad different in the form of a galette—truly the rustic beauty of the baking world. So forgiving and so delicious.

PREP TIME: 20 minutes • **CHILLING TIME:** 15 to 20 minutes • **BAKE TIME:** 55 to 65 minutes
MAKES 1 GALETTE, ABOUT 8 SERVINGS

1. Lay an 18-inch piece of parchment paper on a work surface. Set the pie dough on the parchment paper and roll it out into a 14-inch disc. Place the parchment paper with the pie dough on a sheet pan. Set aside.

2. In a small bowl, combine the shredded cheese and flour. Sprinkle the mixture on the crust, leaving bare a 2-inch border to be folded over the apples.

3. Starting in the middle, arrange the apple slices in overlapping circles on top of the cheese, again leaving the outside 2 inches bare.

4. In a medium bowl, combine the brown sugar, cinnamon, and melted butter.

5. Brush the brown sugar mixture over the apples. Fold the outer 2 inches of the dough over the apples, working your way around and creating pleats as you go. Brush the pleated dough evenly with the egg wash. Sprinkle the turbinado sugar evenly over the entire galette, including the folded-over dough.

6. Chill the galette in the refrigerator for 15 to 20 minutes.

7. When ready to bake, preheat the oven to 350°F.

8. Bake for 55 to 65 minutes, until the apples are tender and the crust is golden and cooked through.

9. Let the galette cool slightly before serving. I highly recommend adding a scoop of vanilla ice cream!

1 recipe Never-Fail Pie Crust (page 239)

1 cup (113 g) shredded cheddar cheese

1 tablespoon all-purpose flour

3 large Honeycrisp apples, cored and cut into 1/8-inch slices with a mandoline

1/4 cup (50 g) packed light brown sugar

1 teaspoon ground cinnamon

2 tablespoons unsalted butter, melted

1 large egg, whisked, for an egg wash

1 tablespoon turbinado sugar (Sugar in the Raw)

CREAM CHEESE POUND CAKE

This is my all-time favorite cake. It never fails. It lends itself beautifully to any frosting (but certainly doesn't need any) and any season. I use cake flour for an extra-delicate crumb.

No cake that has ever come out of my kitchen gets as many compliments as this one does. If you need cake for any occasion, make this!

PREP TIME: 10 minutes • **BAKE TIME:** 1 hour 20 minutes • **MAKES 1 POUND CAKE, ABOUT 12 SERVINGS**

1. Preheat the oven to 325°F. Butter and flour a 10-inch Bundt pan or grease it with nonstick spray.

2. In the bowl of a stand mixer fitted with the paddle attachment or in a large bowl using a handheld mixer, combine the cream cheese and butter on high speed until smooth, about 3 minutes. With the mixer on low, gradually add the granulated sugar. Turn the mixer to high and beat until lighter and fluffier, 2 to 3 minutes. Add the eggs, one at a time, beating well with each addition. Add the vanilla. Add the flour all at once and mix until just combined. Turn the mixer to low speed, add the buttermilk, and mix until just incorporated. Remove the bowl from the stand mixer and scrape the sides with a rubber spatula to get every last bit of the ingredients incorporated.

3. Pour the batter into the prepared pan. Leave at least 1½ inches between the top of the batter and the top edge of the pan. Bake for 1 hour to 1 hour and 20 minutes, checking for doneness at 1 hour. The cake is done when a toothpick inserted into the center of the cake comes out with a few crumbs but no wet batter clinging to it. The cake will be dark golden brown around the edges and lighter in the center.

4. Let the cake cool in the pan until it reaches room temperature. Place a serving plate on top of the pan and carefully flip over so that the cake comes out and rests on the plate. Dust with confectioners' sugar, then cut and serve.

5. Store covered at room temperature for 1 or 2 days or in an airtight container in the refrigerator for 3 or 4 days. To keep Bundt or layer cakes moist at room temperature, secure a piece of bread to the cut side with a toothpick. The bread will get hard, but the cake will stay moist.

Butter and flour or nonstick spray, for the pan

One 8-ounce (227 g) package cream cheese, at room temperature

1¼ cups (2½ sticks / 284 g) salted butter, at room temperature

3 cups (600 g) granulated sugar

6 large eggs, at room temperature

2 teaspoons vanilla extract

3 cups (375 g) cake flour

¼ cup (60 g) buttermilk, at room temperature

Confectioners' sugar, for dusting

NEVER-FAIL PIE CRUST

Everyone says their pie crust is the best. The flakiest. The most tender. I've heard it so many times that I've decided to agree. Food isn't always about the perfect formula; it's often linked to the bonds we create with it from our youth. Pie crust most definitely fits into this category, as we tend to fall in love with what our loved ones made. I won't claim this is the best, but I will verify that it's tender. It's flaky. And it's the perfect complement to any hot or cold pie. Just wait until you try it!

PREP TIME: 20 minutes • **CHILLING TIME:** 1 hour • **BAKE TIME:** depends on recipe • **MAKES ENOUGH DOUGH FOR 1 DOUBLE-CRUST OR 2 SINGLE-CRUST PIES**

1. In the bowl of a food processor, pulse together the flour, sugar, and salt until combined. Add the shortening and pulse until pea-size crumbs form. Transfer the dough to a large bowl.

2. In a small bowl, whisk the egg, vinegar, and ½ cup (120 ml) water. Pour the mixture over the dough and mix until combined. The dough will be sticky. Cover the dough with plastic wrap and chill in the refrigerator for at least 1 hour before rolling.

3. Consult the baking directions for whatever main recipe you're using, but here's how to work with this dough depending on whether the filling needs to be baked or not:

IF THE FILLING NEEDS TO BE BAKED: Divide the chilled dough in half on a generously floured work surface. Roll one half of the dough to a ¼-inch thickness and transfer to a 9-inch pie dish. If you're making a 2-crust pie, roll out the second half of the dough as well. Bake as instructed in the recipe.

IF THE FILLING DOES NOT NEED TO BE BAKED: You'll blind-bake the crust. Transfer the oven rack to the lowest level and preheat the oven to 375°F. Divide the chilled dough in half on a generously floured work surface. Roll one half of the dough to a ¼-inch thickness and transfer to a 9-inch pie dish. Loosely fit a sheet of foil over the unbaked crust and weigh it down with pie weights, uncooked rice, or uncooked beans. Bake for 25 to 30 minutes. Remove the weights and foil, then bake for another 10 to 12 minutes, until golden brown. Fill and chill according to the recipe.

4. For either baking method, wrap any remaining dough in plastic wrap and store in the refrigerator for 3 or 4 days.

4 cups (500 g) all-purpose flour

1 tablespoon granulated sugar

1½ teaspoons kosher salt

1½ cups (308 g) vegetable shortening

1 large egg, beaten

1 tablespoon white vinegar

WHITE CAKE WITH WHIPPED VANILLA BUTTERCREAM

This is the cake that will boost you to "legendary" status among friends and family. This is the cake that people will love to look at but love to eat even more. This is the cake that will make you the most popular baker in the neighborhood. This is the cake that everyone will talk about—all the time. It's just that good!

PREP TIME: 20 minutes • **BAKE TIME:** 27 to 30 minutes • **MAKES 1 LAYER CAKE, ABOUT 8 SERVINGS**

1. Preheat the oven to 350°F. Grease two 8-inch round cake pans with nonstick spray or fit parchment rounds into the bottoms of the pans.

2. In a medium bowl, combine the milk, egg whites, and extracts and whisk with a fork until blended. Set aside.

3. In the bowl of a stand mixer fitted with the paddle attachment, mix together the cake flour, sugar, baking powder, and salt on low speed. Add the cubed butter and continue beating on low until all the butter is incorporated, 2 to 3 minutes. Add all but ½ cup of the milk mixture to the flour mixture and beat on medium speed for 1½ minutes, or until fully combined. Add the remaining ½ cup milk mixture and beat for about 1 minute, until fully combined.

4. Divide the batter evenly between the two prepared cake pans (approximately 2¾ cups of batter per pan).

5. Bake for 27 to 30 minutes. The cake is done when a toothpick inserted into the center comes out with a few crumbs but has no wet batter clinging to it.

6. Let the cake layers cool in the pans for about 5 minutes, then invert them onto a wire rack to cool completely.

7. Place the first layer on a cake plate and frost with the vanilla buttercream. Place the second layer on top, frost the sides and top, and serve.

8. Cover the cake and store at room temperature for 1 or 2 days or in an airtight container in the refrigerator for 3 or 4 days.

Nonstick spray or parchment paper

1 cup (240 ml) whole milk, at room temperature

6 large (197 g) egg whites, at room temperature

2 teaspoons almond extract

1 teaspoon vanilla extract

2¼ cups (261 g) cake flour

1¾ cups (350 g) granulated sugar

4 teaspoons baking powder

1 teaspoon kosher salt

¾ cup (1½ sticks / 170 g) unsalted butter, softened but still cool, cut into ½-inch cubes

Whipped Vanilla Buttercream (recipe follows)

Whipped Vanilla Buttercream

PREP TIME: 5 minutes • **MIXING TIME:** 10 to 13 minutes • **MAKES ABOUT 4 CUPS FROSTING**

½ pound (2 sticks / 227 g) unsalted butter, at room temperature

2 teaspoons vanilla extract

1 teaspoon almond extract

4 cups (500 g) confectioners' sugar

2 tablespoons whole milk or up to ½ cup (120 ml) for a loose, creamy consistency

Pinch of kosher salt

1. In the bowl of a stand mixer fitted with the whisk attachment or in a large bowl using a handheld whisk, beat the butter on medium-high speed until light and fluffy, about 3 minutes. Add the vanilla and almond extracts. With the mixer on low, slowly add in the confectioners' sugar, milk, and salt until incorporated, frequently scraping the sides and bottom of the bowl. Turn the mixer to high and whip the frosting for at least 3 minutes, until the frosting is fluffier and creamy. (My mixer went for 7 minutes.) If the frosting is too thick to spread, gradually beat in additional milk 1 tablespoon at a time.

2. Store in an airtight container in the refrigerator for up to 2 weeks. Re-whip on high speed in the stand mixer before using.

YELLOW CAKE WITH CHOCOLATE FROSTING

Or "birthday cake," as I knew it growing up. I didn't know there were other flavors of birthday cake, just yellow cake with chocolate frosting. No complaints here—it is a magical combination. Soft, moist, buttery cake with a smooth and rich chocolate buttercream. Isn't it wonderful that as an adult you don't need a special occasion to make a cake? You can just treat yourself!
See the photo on pages 244–245.

PREP TIME: 20 minutes • **BAKE TIME:** 20 to 25 minutes • **MAKES 1 LAYER CAKE, ABOUT 8 SERVINGS**

1. Preheat the oven to 350°F. Grease two 8-inch round cake pans with nonstick spray or fit parchment rounds into the bottoms of the pans.

2. Sift together the flour, sugar, baking powder, and salt into a large bowl. Set aside.

3. In the bowl of a stand mixer fitted with the paddle attachment or in a large bowl using a handheld mixer, cream the butter on medium speed until light and fluffy, 1 to 2 minutes. Add the flour mixture and mix on low for 30 seconds. Add the milk, oil, vanilla, and eggs and mix on medium-high until fully combined, about 1 minute.

4. Divide the batter between the prepared pans (about 2¼ cups of batter per pan).

5. Bake for 20 to 25 minutes. The cake is done when a toothpick inserted into the center comes out with a few crumbs but has no wet batter clinging to it. Let the cake layers cool in the pans for about 5 minutes, then invert them onto a wire rack to cool completely.

6. Place the first layer on a cake plate and frost with chocolate buttercream. Place the second layer on top, frost the sides and top, and serve.

7. Cover the cake and store at room temperature for 1 or 2 days. It can also be stored in an airtight container in the refrigerator for 3 or 4 days.

Nonstick spray or parchment paper

2¼ cups (281 g) all-purpose flour

1½ cups (300 g) granulated sugar

3½ teaspoons baking powder

1 teaspoon kosher salt

½ cup (1 stick / 114 g) unsalted butter, at room temperature

1¼ cups (300 ml) whole milk, at room temperature

2 tablespoons vegetable oil

1 tablespoon vanilla extract

3 large eggs, at room temperature

Chocolate Buttercream (page 250)

YELLOW CAKE WITH CHOCOLATE FROSTING, PAGE 243

YELLOW CAKE WITH CHOCOLATE FROSTING, PAGE 243

CHOCOLATE CAKE WITH CHOCOLATE FROSTING

Everyone should have at their disposal a recipe for the perfect chocolate cake. It should be moist, flavorful, and, most important, moist. Yes, I know I said *moist* twice, but I truly can't think of anything worse than dry chocolate cake. This batter may fool you, as it will be very runny going into the pans, but it will bake up beautifully every time.

PREP TIME: 20 minutes • **BAKE TIME:** 30 to 40 minutes • **COOLING TIME:** 30 minutes •
MAKES ONE 2-LAYER CAKE, ABOUT 12 SERVINGS

1. Preheat the oven to 350°F. Grease two 8-inch round cake pans with nonstick spray or fit parchment rounds into the bottoms of the pans.

2. Sift together the flour, sugar, cocoa powder, baking soda, baking powder, and salt into a large bowl and whisk until combined.

3. In a medium bowl and using a handheld mixer, mix together the buttermilk, oil, eggs, and vanilla on low speed until combined. Slowly add the wet mixture into the dry. Add the coffee and stir just to combine, using a spatula to scrape the bottom of the bowl as needed.

4. Divide the batter between the prepared pans (about 2½ cups batter per pan) and bake for 30 to 40 minutes. The cake is done when a toothpick inserted into the center comes out with a few crumbs but no wet batter clinging to it.

5. Let the cakes cool in the pans for about 30 minutes, then invert them onto a wire rack to cool completely.

6. Place the first layer on a cake plate and frost with the chocolate buttercream. Place the second layer on top, frost the sides and top, and serve.

7. Cover the cake and store at room temperature for 1 or 2 days. It can also be stored in an airtight container in the refrigerator for 3 or 4 days.

Nonstick spray or parchment paper

1¾ cups (219 g) all-purpose flour

2 cups (400 g) granulated sugar

¾ cup (90 g) unsweetened cocoa powder

2 teaspoons baking soda

1 teaspoon baking powder

1 teaspoon kosher salt

1 cup (240 g) buttermilk, at room temperature

½ cup (120 ml) vegetable oil

2 extra-large eggs, at room temperature

2 teaspoons vanilla extract

1 cup (240 ml) freshly brewed hot coffee

Chocolate Buttercream (recipe follows)

Chocolate Buttercream

PREP TIME: 5 minutes • **MIXING TIME:** 10 minutes • **MAKES ABOUT 4 CUPS FROSTING**

1½ cups (3 sticks / 341 g) unsalted butter, at room temperature

4 cups (500 g) confectioners' sugar

¾ cup (94 g) unsweetened cocoa powder

2 teaspoons vanilla extract

Pinch of table salt

4 tablespoons (60 g) heavy whipping cream

1. In the bowl of a stand mixer fitted with the whisk attachment or in a large bowl using a handheld whisk, whisk the butter and confectioners' sugar on medium-high speed until very pale and fluffy, about 5 minutes. Stop at least once to scrape the bowl.

2. With the mixer off, add the cocoa powder, vanilla, and salt. Turn the mixer on low and blend for about 30 seconds. With the mixer running, add the heavy cream, a tablespoon at a time. When all the cream has been added and the mixture is mostly combined, remove the bowl from the mixer and scrape down the sides with a rubber spatula.

3. Turn the mixer to medium-high and mix for 3 to 5 minutes, until the frosting is lighter and fluffier. It will be shiny and seem to have many large air bubbles throughout, and this is exactly what we are going for. (You can smooth the air bubbles out on the cake if so desired.) Store in an airtight container in the refrigerator for 3 to 5 days.

SALTED CARAMEL BANANA CAKE

This cake is so good you will *peel* it in your bones. I love it a *bunch*. Practically *bananas* for it! You may not want to *split* it with family and friends. Okay, I'll stop with the banana puns. Puns might not be *appealing* to everyone. I'll stop now, promise.

Want to know the real deal about this cake? It's loaded with banana flavor and perfectly complemented by the salted caramel frosting. It's soft, moist, loaded with banana deliciousness, and one of those desserts that you wish weren't dessert because you want to eat it the second you see it on the counter in the morning. If you sneak a bite for breakfast, no worries—I've done it, too, and it was worth it.

PREP TIME: 15 minutes • **BAKE TIME:** 25 to 28 minutes • **MAKES 8 SERVINGS**

1. Preheat the oven to 350°F. Grease two 8-inch round cake pans with nonstick spray or fit parchment rounds into the bottoms of the pans.

2. Using a hand mixer on high speed, in a large bowl beat the butter and brown sugar until airy and creamy, about 2 minutes. On low speed, add the vanilla and mix until incorporated. Add the eggs and mix on low until incorporated. Add the flour and salt and mix well. Fold in the mashed bananas.

3. Divide the batter between the prepared pans and bake for 25 to 28 minutes. The cake is done when a toothpick inserted into the center comes out with a few crumbs but no wet batter clinging to it.

4. Let the cakes cool in the pans for 5 minutes, then carefully invert them onto a wire rack to cool completely.

5. Place the first layer on a cake plate and frost with salted caramel buttercream. Place the second layer on top, frost the sides and top, and serve.

6. Store the cake covered at room temperature for 1 or 2 days or in an airtight container in the refrigerator for 3 or 4 days. To keep Bundt or layer cakes moist at room temperature, secure a piece of bread to the cut side with a toothpick. The bread will get hard, but the cake will stay moist.

Nonstick spray or parchment paper

1 cup (2 sticks / 227 g) unsalted butter, melted

2 cups (400 g) packed light brown sugar

1 tablespoon vanilla extract

2 large eggs, at room temperature

2 cups (250 g) all-purpose flour

1 teaspoon kosher salt

2 medium ripe bananas, mashed (about ⅔ cup / 200 g; some chunks okay)

Salted Caramel Buttercream (recipe follows)

Salted Caramel Buttercream

PREP TIME: 5 minutes • **MIXING TIME:** 4 minutes • **MAKES ABOUT 2½ CUPS FROSTING**

8 tablespoons (1 stick / 114 g) unsalted butter, at room temperature

2 cups (250 g) confectioners' sugar, sifted

½ teaspoon table salt

¼ cup (82 g) packaged caramel topping

1½ teaspoons whole milk, as needed

1. In the bowl of a stand mixer fitted with the paddle attachment or in a large bowl using a handheld mixer, combine the butter, confectioners' sugar, salt, and caramel topping on low speed until the sugar well incorporated, 1 to 2 minutes.

2. Increase the speed to high and beat until smooth and fluffy, about 2 minutes. If the frosting is thick, add the milk ½ teaspoon at a time to reach desired consistency. Store in an airtight container in the refrigerator for 3 to 5 days.

APPLE BUNDT CAKE

There is a shortage of perfect apple cakes in the world; it would be a pity to damage this one. (Point if you can get the vague movie reference there!) Truly, though, this is a perfect cake—one that is delectable all year long but most especially in the fall when the temperatures are beginning to cool down.

PREP TIME: 15 minutes • **BAKE TIME:** 1 hour 10 minutes • **COOLING TIME:** 20 minutes •
MAKES 1 BUNDT CAKE, ABOUT 12 SERVINGS

1. **MAKE THE CAKE:** Preheat the oven to 325°F. Grease a 9-inch Bundt pan with nonstick spray.

2. In a large bowl, beat the granulated sugar, oil, vanilla, and eggs with a handheld mixer on medium speed until light and fluffy, about 2 minutes.

3. Sift together the flour, baking soda, cinnamon, and salt into a medium bowl. Add the dry ingredients to the wet and stir until just combined. Fold in the apples.

4. Pour the batter into the prepared pan and bake for 55 to 70 minutes. The cake is done when a toothpick inserted into the center comes out with a few crumbs but no wet batter clinging to it.

5. Let the cake cool in the pan for about 20 minutes, then invert it onto a serving platter or cake stand.

6. **MAKE THE CARAMEL GLAZE:** Heat the butter, heavy cream, and brown sugar in a small saucepan over medium heat. Bring to a boil, stirring to dissolve the sugar, then remove from the heat. Add the vanilla and stir until combined. Let sit 5 to 10 minutes to thicken.

7. Drizzle the glaze over the warm cake. Serve warm.

8. Store the cake covered at room temperature for 1 or 2 days or in an airtight container in the refrigerator for 3 or 4 days. To keep Bundt or layer cakes moist at room temperature, secure a piece of bread to the cut side with a toothpick. The bread will get hard, but the cake will stay moist.

CAKE

Nonstick spray

2 cups (400 g) granulated sugar

1½ cups (360 ml) vegetable oil

2 teaspoons vanilla extract

3 large eggs, at room temperature

3 cups (375 g) all-purpose flour

1 teaspoon baking soda

1 teaspoon ground cinnamon

1 teaspoon kosher salt

3 medium Granny Smith apples, peeled, cored, and cut into ½-inch dice

CARAMEL GLAZE

½ cup (1 stick / 114 g) unsalted butter

2 teaspoons heavy cream

½ cup (100 g) packed light brown sugar

1 teaspoon vanilla extract

CHOCOLATE BEER CAKE

I have a rule in my test kitchen, and that is if you open a beer for a recipe you have to drink a beer. Best rule ever. I tested this recipe for a solid three days before creating this perfect concoction, and let me just tell you, it was the funnest recipe testing ever. This was supposed to be beer bread, but the consistency is so cake-like that I had to call it a cake. If you love beer bread, it's a must try!

PREP TIME: 10 minutes • **BAKE TIME:** 25 minutes • **MAKES 1 SKILLET CAKE, ABOUT 12 SERVINGS**

1. Preheat the oven to 350°F. Grease a 10-inch oven-safe skillet with nonstick spray.

2. In a large bowl, combine the flour, cocoa powder, baking powder, salt, brown sugar, and ½ cup of the chocolate chunks. Mix together with a fork. Add the beer and continue mixing with the fork until just combined.

3. Pour the mixture into the prepared skillet. Top with the pats of butter. Sprinkle the remaining ½ cup chocolate chunks on top.

4. Bake for 25 minutes, or until a toothpick inserted into the center comes out with a few crumbs but no wet batter clinging to it.

5. Let cool in the skillet, then cut into wedges and serve.

6. Store the cake covered at room temperature for 1 or 2 days or in an airtight container in the refrigerator for 3 or 4 days.

Nonstick spray

2½ cups (313 g) all-purpose flour

½ cup (59 g) unsweetened cocoa powder

1 tablespoon baking powder

½ teaspoon kosher salt

½ cup (100 g) packed light brown sugar

1 cup (168 g) milk chocolate or semi-sweet chocolate chunks

One 12-ounce (360 ml) bottle of beer, at room temperature (I prefer Miller Lite)

½ cup (1 stick / 114 g) cold unsalted butter, cut into 12 pats

SIMPLY THE MOISTEST CHOCOLATE CAKE

Based on a super-popular childhood treat, this cake is guaranteed to bring you that elusive joy sparked by memories. But on the off chance you never had Ding-Dongs growing up, no worries. It's a rich chocolate cake with a glorious filling as soft as ermine. Then it's covered in a smooth and glossy chocolate ganache. Big fancy words, but they match that big fancy flavor. *See the photo on page 260.*

PREP TIME: 20 minutes • **COOK TIME:** 20 to 25 minutes • **MAKES 1 SHEET CAKE, ABOUT 12 SERVINGS**

CHOCOLATE CAKE

1¾ cups (219 g) all-purpose flour

2 cups (400 g) granulated sugar

¾ cup (90 g) good-quality unsweetened cocoa powder

2 teaspoons baking soda

1 teaspoon baking powder

1 teaspoon kosher salt

1 cup (240 ml) buttermilk, at room temperature

½ cup (120 ml) vegetable oil

2 extra-large eggs, at room temperature

2 teaspoons vanilla extract

1 cup (240 ml) freshly brewed hot coffee

FILLING

1 cup (240 ml) whole milk

5 tablespoons (39 g) all-purpose flour

1 teaspoon vanilla extract

1 cup (2 sticks / 227 g) unsalted butter

1 cup (200 g) sugar

1. Preheat the oven to 350°F. Line a rimmed 13 × 18-inch pan (half sheet pan) with parchment paper. Make sure the parchment extends over two sides of the pan so you can use it to lift out the cake when it is ready to be assembled.

2. **MAKE THE CAKE:** Into the bowl of a large stand mixer fitted with the whisk attachment, sift together the flour, sugar, cocoa powder, baking soda, baking powder, and salt. Turn the mixer on low and whisk the dry ingredients until incorporated, about 30 seconds. Turn off the mixer, remove the whisk attachment, and add the paddle attachment.

3. In a medium bowl, combine the buttermilk, oil, eggs, and vanilla.

4. Turn the mixer to low and slowly add the buttermilk mixture, mixing until combined. With the mixer still on low, add the coffee and stir just until combined. Turn off the mixer and scrape the bottom of the bowl with a rubber spatula as needed.

5. Pour the batter evenly into the prepared sheet pan. Bake for 20 to 25 minutes. The cake is done when a toothpick inserted into the center comes out with a few crumbs but has no wet batter clinging to it.

6. Let the cake cool in the pan for about 15 minutes, then place in the freezer as you prepare the filling.

7. **MAKE THE FILLING:** Pour the milk into a small saucepan over medium heat. Whisk in the flour until no lumps remain. Turn the heat to medium-low and bring to a simmer, stirring continuously, until the mixture is thick, like a roux. Remove from the heat, stir in the vanilla, and set aside to cool completely.

8. Using a handheld mixer, in a medium bowl cream the butter and sugar on medium-high speed until fluffy, about 8 minutes. Add the milk mixture and beat until the mixture resembles whipped cream.

9. **MAKE THE GANACHE:** Place the chopped chocolate in a large bowl.

10. Pour the heavy cream in a quart-size microwave-safe bowl. Microwave on high for 3 to 4 minutes, until it just begins to simmer. Be careful not to let the cream boil over.

11. Pour the cream over the chopped chocolate and let stand for at least 2 minutes so that it can thicken. After 2 minutes, stir until no lumps remain. Set aside the ganache to cool completely.

12. **ASSEMBLE THE CAKE:** Carefully lift the cake out of the pan using the overhanging parchment paper as a sling. Cut the cake exactly in half crosswise with a sharp knife.

13. Place one half of the cake on a serving plate (I like to use a clean sheet pan) and cover with the prepared filling. Place the other half of the cake on top of the filling.

14. Pour the ganache over the cake. Serve immediately or refrigerate until ready to serve.

GANACHE

One 8-ounce bar (227 g) semi-sweet chocolate, finely chopped

1 cup (240 ml) heavy cream, at room temperature

SIMPLY THE MOISTEST CHOCOLATE CAKE, PAGE 258

CHOCOLATE PULL-APART BREAD, PAGE 262

CHOCOLATE PULL-APART BREAD

This is a pretty extravagant recipe for a homestead book. You can absolutely just make the chocolate bread on its own, without the filling. It has a subtle chocolate flavor and isn't overly sweet—it is ideal for French toast, toasted with jam, or even as a snack. After mastering the chocolate bread, I knew I wanted to make it into a dessert—so I added more chocolate, marshmallow, and cherries. It's a beautiful mess, loaded with sweetness, and the perfect way to add some unexpected delight to people's lives!
See the photo on page 261.

PREP TIME: 25 minutes • **RESTING TIME:** 2 hours • **BAKE TIME:** 20 minutes •
MAKES 1 LOAF, ABOUT 12 SERVINGS

CHOCOLATE BREAD

¼ cup (60 ml) warm water (105°F to 115°F)

2¼ teaspoons (1 packet) active dry yeast

1 teaspoon granulated sugar

1 cup (240 ml) brewed coffee, cooled

4 tablespoons (½ stick / 57 g) unsalted butter, melted and cooled

1 large egg, at room temperature, separated

3½ cups (438 g) all-purpose flour, plus more as needed

½ cup (59 g) unsweetened cocoa powder

½ cup (100 g) packed light brown sugar

1½ teaspoons kosher salt

⅓ cup (56 g) semi-sweet chocolate chips

Canola oil, for greasing

2 teaspoons turbinado sugar

1. **MAKE THE CHOCOLATE BREAD:** In a small bowl, combine the warm water, yeast, and sugar. Mix, then let rest until foamy, about 5 minutes. Set aside.

2. In a medium bowl, whisk the coffee, butter, and egg yolk. Set aside. Reserve the egg white in the refrigerator for the egg wash in step 9.

3. In the bowl of a stand mixer fitted with the whisk attachment or in a large bowl using a handheld whisk, whisk 3 cups of the flour, the cocoa powder, brown sugar, and salt on low speed until combined, about 30 seconds. Turn off the mixer and remove the whisk attachment.

4. Add the yeast mixture, then add the butter mixture and the chocolate chips to the flour mixture. Using the dough hook attachment, knead on low until the dough comes together, about 4 minutes. Add the remaining ½ cup flour, a tablespoon at a time, if the dough still seems sticky. (If you're kneading by hand, turn the dough out onto a lightly floured surface and knead for about 10 minutes, until smooth and elastic. Add the remaining flour, a tablespoon at a time, to keep the dough from being too sticky.) Shape the dough into a ball.

5. Place the dough in a large oiled bowl. Flip over the dough, making sure all sides are covered in the oil. Cover the dough with a kitchen towel. Let the dough rise in a warm draft-free area until doubled in size, about 1 hour.

6. Line a sheet pan with parchment paper. Punch the dough, turn it out onto a floured surface, and divide it evenly in half. Reshape each half into a ball by tucking the sides under. Place the dough rounds onto the prepared sheet pan with at least 3 inches between them, cover with a towel, and let rise for 1 hour, or until doubled in size.

7. When ready to bake, preheat the oven to 375°F.

8. Score the top of each loaf with a sharp serrated knife. Make three or four shallow cuts (about ¼ inch deep) in each.

9. In a small dish, whisk the reserved egg white with a teaspoon of water. Brush the tops of both loaves with the egg wash and sprinkle with the turbinado sugar.

10. Bake for 20 minutes, or until the tops of the loaves are crusty.

11. Remove from the oven and let cool to room temperature.

12. **MAKE THE FILLING:** When the chocolate bread is completely cool, slice each loaf horizontally and vertically in a crisscross pattern into 1-inch-square sections, taking care not to slice all the way through the loaves. You want individual cubes that are about 1-inch tall but that are still attached to the bread.

13. Fill a piping bag or a quart-size resealable plastic bag with a corner cut off with the hot fudge and pipe it into the grooves in the bread. Fill a second piping bag with the marshmallow fluff and pipe into the grooves.

14. Place the filled loaves of bread back in the oven to broil for 3 to 5 minutes, until the marshmallow has toasted. Watch closely so it doesn't burn. Top with the chopped peanuts and maraschino cherries.

15. This is best served warm. Let the kids dive in and pull out individual sections of the hot fudge and marshmallow-covered chocolate bread. It will be messy and delightful!

FILLING

½ cup (152 g) hot fudge

1 cup (80 g) marshmallow fluff

¼ cup (38 g) roughly chopped peanuts

Maraschino cherries, for garnish

Puppy Chow

We grew up calling this puppy chow, but it's definitely not dog food! Some folks know it as muddie buddies, muddy munch, or reindeer chow—and I know there are many more names! Whatever you call it, you can add *delicious*, because it is. These recipes are my own special take on it, like adding bacon. It sounds crazy, as most traditional Minnesota dishes do, but it is good. So good!

SNICKERDOODLE PUPPY CHOW

NOTE: You can easily double these recipes. Just make sure you have a large enough bowl to mix the ingredients in and that you work in batches when coating the cereal with chocolate.

TRADITIONAL PUPPY CHOW

BACON PUPPY CHOW

SMORES PUPPY CHOW

TRADITIONAL PUPPY CHOW

PREP TIME: 10 minutes • **MAKES 12 SERVINGS**

1 cup (170 g) semi-sweet chocolate chips

½ cup (125 g) creamy peanut butter

4 tablespoons (½ stick / 57 g) unsalted butter

1 teaspoon vanilla extract

6 cups (282 g) Rice Chex cereal

2 cups (250 g) confectioners' sugar

1. Place the chocolate chips, peanut butter, and butter in a medium microwave-safe bowl. Microwave in 30-second intervals, stirring in between. Continue until the mixture is smooth when stirred.

2. Mix in the vanilla extract.

3. Pour the cereal into a large bowl. Add the chocolate mixture and gently stir until cereal is evenly coated. Pour the coated cereal into a large resealable plastic bag. Add the confectioners' sugar. Seal the bag and shake until the cereal is well coated. Spread on parchment paper or waxed paper. Let sit until cool and the chocolate is set.

4. Store the puppy chow in an airtight container at room temperature for 3 or 4 days or in the refrigerator for up to 2 weeks.

SNICKERDOODLE PUPPY CHOW

PREP TIME: 10 minutes   •   **MAKES 12 SERVINGS**

1. Place the almond bark in a small microwave-safe bowl. Microwave in 30-second intervals, stirring in between. Stir in the granulated sugar.

2. Pour the cereal into a large bowl and pour the almond bark mixture over the top. With a spatula, stir well, making sure every piece is coated.

3. Pour the cereal into a large resealable plastic bag and sprinkle the confectioners' sugar and cinnamon on top. Close the bag and shake until well coated.

4. Spread the mixture evenly on a sheet pan and allow to set.

5. Store the puppy chow in an airtight container at room temperature for 3 or 4 days or in the refrigerator for up to 2 weeks.

8 ounces (227 g) almond bark

2 tablespoons granulated sugar

6 cups (282 g) Rice Chex cereal

2 teaspoons ground cinnamon

½ cup (63 g) confectioners' sugar

BACON PUPPY CHOW

PREP TIME: 10 minutes • **COOK TIME:** 20 minutes • **MAKES 12 SERVINGS**

BACON

8 slices (120 g) thick-cut bacon

¼ cup (60 ml) pure maple syrup

2 tablespoons packed light brown sugar

⅛ teaspoon cayenne pepper

½ teaspoon freshly ground black pepper

CEREAL

8 ounces (227 g) almond bark

1 cup (250 g) creamy peanut butter

6 cups (282 g) Rice Chex cereal

½ cup (63 g) confectioners' sugar

1. **COOK THE BACON:** Preheat the oven to 425°F. Line a sheet pan with parchment paper or foil.

2. Lay the bacon slices on the prepared sheet pan. In a medium bowl, mix the syrup, brown sugar, cayenne, and black pepper. Mix well. Brush both sides of the bacon slices with the maple mixture.

3. Bake for 20 minutes, or until crispy.

4. Set the cooked bacon on a plate lined with paper towels to drain and cool. Crumble the cooled bacon into bite-size pieces.

5. **MIX THE CEREAL:** Place the almond bark in a medium microwave-safe bowl. Microwave in 30-second intervals, stirring in between, until fully melted. Stir in the peanut butter until melted in.

6. Pour the cereal into a large bowl and pour the almond bark mixture on top. With a spatula, stir well, making sure every piece of cereal is coated.

7. **ASSEMBLE THE CHOW:** Pour the coated cereal, crumbled bacon, and confectioners' sugar into a large resealable plastic bag. Close the bag and shake until well coated.

8. Spread the mixture evenly on a sheet pan and let set.

9. Store the puppy chow in an airtight container in the refrigerator for up to 2 weeks.

SMORES PUPPY CHOW

PREP TIME: 10 minutes • **MAKES 12 SERVINGS**

1. Place 2 cups of the Golden Grahams cereal, the Rice Chex cereal, and 1 cup of the mini marshmallows in a large bowl.

2. Place the chocolate chips and peanut butter in a small microwave-safe bowl. Microwave in 30-second intervals, stirring in between. Usually 1 minute is enough.

3. Pour the melted mixture over the cereal and marshmallows and stir with a spatula until everything is coated.

4. Carefully pour the mixture into a large resealable plastic bag. Add the confectioners' sugar and seal the bag. Shake until every piece is coated in sugar.

5. Open the plastic bag and add in the remaining ½ cup Golden Grahams and remaining ½ cup mini marshmallows. Shake the bag again to just barely coat the add-ins.

6. Pour into a bowl and serve.

7. Store the puppy chow in an airtight container at room temperature for 3 or 4 days or in the refrigerator for up to 2 weeks.

2½ cups (105 g) Golden Grahams cereal

2 cups (66 g) Rice Chex cereal

1½ cups (75 g) mini marshmallows

½ cup milk chocolate chips

¼ cup (62 g) creamy peanut butter

1 cup (125 g) confectioners' sugar

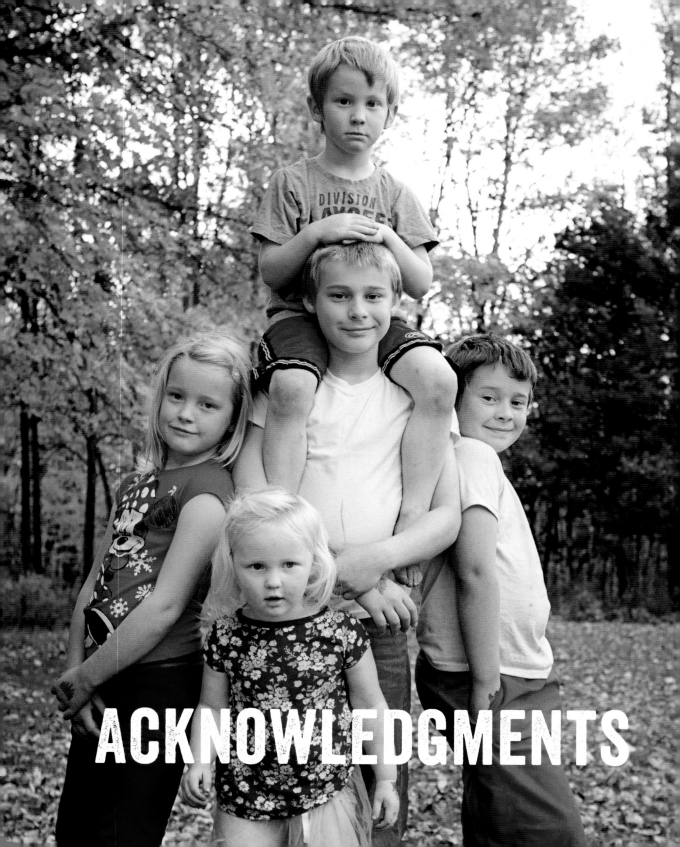

ACKNOWLEDGMENTS

Chad, Colton, Parker, Audrey, Eddie, and Olivia

I LOVE YOU GUYS. So much. I know the exact moments when you made me a better person—and those memories are as precious to me as anything. Thanks for putting up with my long hours and never-ending work and being the best taste testers ever. Thanks for getting my weird personality and laughing with me. Thanks for being kind humans who make the world a better place. You are my everything.

Autumn

Thanks for being my work and life COO. Glad one of us has got it together. And thanks for always striving for bigger! twss

Liz

You made my life better by being in it—always so in awe of your talents! If Nashville ever finds out about you, I am toast.

Cassie

Thanks for being the best at what you do! This book would be scribbled incoherently on a paper towel and laminated for presentation if it wasn't for you (and your amazing team!).

Alison

I have known you almost a decade now and just want to apologize for that. Ha! You are the best person I have in my corner, and I am super grateful for your willingness to fight for me, no matter what!

Readers

Some of you have been following along on my journey for over a decade, and that's amazing to me. You have accepted me without filter, at my lowest moments, and at my highest, and most definitely have laughed alongside me. You have never failed to offer up encouragement and hope. I literally would not be at this crazy place in time without you. I am forever grateful.

UNIVERSAL CONVERSION CHART

OVEN TEMPERATURE EQUIVALENTS

250°F = 120°C

275°F = 135°C

300°F = 150°C

325°F = 160°C

350°F = 180°C

375°F = 190°C

400°F = 200°C

425°F = 220°C

450°F = 230°C

475°F = 240°C

500°F = 260°C

MEASUREMENT EQUIVALENTS

Measurements should always be level unless directed otherwise.

⅛ teaspoon = 0.5 mL

¼ teaspoon = 1 mL

½ teaspoon = 2 mL

1 teaspoon = 5 mL

1 tablespoon = 3 teaspoons = ½ fluid ounce = 15 mL

2 tablespoons = ⅛ cup = 1 fluid ounce = 30 mL

4 tablespoons = ¼ cup = 2 fluid ounces = 60 mL

5⅓ tablespoons = ⅓ cup = 3 fluid ounces = 80 mL

8 tablespoons = ½ cup = 4 fluid ounces = 120 mL

10⅔ tablespoons = ⅔ cup = 5 fluid ounces = 160 mL

12 tablespoons = ¾ cup = 6 fluid ounces = 180 mL

16 tablespoons = 1 cup = 8 fluid ounces = 240 mL

INDEX

HarperCollins books may be purchased for educational, business, or sales promotional use. For information, please email the Special Markets Department at SPsales@harpercollins.com.

FIRST EDITION

Designed by Michelle Crowe

All photographs by the author, except for the following by Breanna Mellem: ii, vi, xii, xiii, xiv, xv, xvi, 34, 46, 100, 158, 176, 185, 196, 246, 247, 270, 271, and 276

Library of Congress Cataloging-in-Publication Data has been applied for.

ISBN 978-0-06-300820-5

22 23 24 25 26   TC   10 9 8 7 6 5 4 3 2 1